Gita and Gospel

GITA

AND

GOSPEL.

BY

NEIL ALEXANDER.

Calcutta :

THACKER, SPINK & CO.

1903

CALCUTTA :
PRINTED BY THACKER, SPINK AND CO.

SI
A

TABLE OF CONTENTS.

ABBREVIATIONS.

AMALNERKAR   ...Amalnerkar, *Priority of the Vedanta-Sutras over the Bhagavadgītā*.

BOSE, *H. C.*   ...Bose, *Hindu Civilization under British Rule*.

DEUSSEN   ...Deussen, *Sechzig Upanishad's des Veda*.

DUTT, *C. A. I*   ...Dutt, *Civilization in Ancient India*.

G.   .. *The Gītā*.

GARBE   ...Garbe, *The Philosophy of Ancient India*.

GOUGH   ...Gough, *The Philosophy of the Upanishads*.

HOPKINS, *R I*   ...Hopkins, *The Religions of India*.

HOPKINS, *G. E. I.*   ...Hopkins, *The Great Epic of India*.

KAEGI   ...Kaegi, *The Rigveda* (Arrowsmith's translation).

KIDD, *P. W. C.*   ...Kidd, *Principles of Western Civilization*.

KRISHNACHARITRA   ...Bunkim Chundra Chatterji, *Krishnacharitra*, fourth edition.

MACDONELL   ...Macdonell, *Sanskrit Literature*.

MOMMSEN   ...Mommsen, *History of Rome*.

MONIER-WILLIAMS   ...Monier-Williams, *Brahmanism and Hinduism*.

MÜLLER, *A. S. L.*   ...Muller, *Ancient Sanskrit Literature*, second edition.

MULLER, *S. S. I. P.*   ...Muller, *Six Systems of Indian Philosophy*.

S. B. E.   ...*The Sacred Books of the East*.

SCHÜRER, *H. J. P.*   ...Schurer, *History of the Jewish People in the Time of Jesus Christ*.

SEAL   ...Brajendra Nath Seal, *Comparative Studies in Vaishnavism and Christianity*.

TELANG   ...Telang, *The Bhagavadgītā, &c.* (Sacred Books of the East, vol. VIII.)

WEBER, *I. I*   ...Weber, *Indian Literature*

CHAPTER I.

WHAT IS THE *BHAGAVADGITA* ?

IN the whole literature of the world there are few poems worthy of comparison, either in point of general interest, or of practical influence, with the *Bhagavadgītā* It is a philosophical work, yet fresh and readable as poetry ; a book of devotion, yet drawing its main inspiration from speculative systems ; a dramatic scene from the most fateful battle of early Indian story, yet breathing the leisure and the subtleties of the schools ; founded on a metaphysical theory originally atheistic,[1] yet teaching the most reverent adoration of the Lord of all : where shall we find a more fascinating study ? Then its influence on educated India has been and still is without a rival. Everybody praises the Upanishads, but very few read them ; here and there one finds a student who turns the pages of a Sūtra or looks into Sankara or Rāmānuja, but the most are content to believe without seeing. The *Gītā*, on the other hand, is read and loved by every educated man. Nor is there any need to apologize for this partiality . the Divine Song is the loveliest flower in the garden of Sanskrit literature.

For the Western mind also the poem has many attractions. The lofty sublimity to which it so often rises, the practical character of much of its teaching, the enthusiastic devotion to the one Lord which breathes through it, and the numerous resemblances it shows to the words of Christ, fill it with unusual interest for men of the West. But while it has many points of affinity with the thought and the religion of Europe, it is nevertheless a genuine

---

[1] The philosophic basis of the book is primarily the *Sānkhya* system which is essentially atheistic.

pioduct of the soil ;[1] indeed it is all the more fit to represent the genius of India that its thought and its poetry are lofty enough to draw the eyes of the West.

What, then, is the *Gītā* ? Can we find our way to the fountain whence the clear stream flows?

A When the dwelling-place of the ancient Aryan tribes was partly on the outer, partly on the inner, side of the Indus (primeval patronymic of both India and her religion), and the tribesmen were equally at home on the farm and on the battle-field, then it was that the mass of the lyrics that form the *Rigveda* were made. We need not stay to set forth the various ways in which this unique body of poetry is of value to modern thought. For us it is of interest because it gives us the earliest glimpse of the religion of the Indo-Aryans. That religion is polytheistic and naturalistic The Vedic hymns laud the powers of nature and natural phenomena as personal gods. They praise also, as distinct powers, the departed fathers. Such is undoubtedly the general character of the religion of that age. On the other hand, the hymns to Varuna bring us very near monotheism indeed.[2]

It is, however, only at a later period when the Aryan conquest had moved out of the Punjab to the South and West, and just on the eve of the formation of the *Rigveda* as a collection of religious hymns, that we find the beginnings of philosophic speculation.[3] A few hymns, chiefly in the tenth Mondôl, ask questions about the origin of the universe, and venture some naive guesses on that tremendous subject. Some of the hymns[4] take for granted the existence of primeval matter, and ask how or by whom it was transformed into a *cosmos*. In others[5] there is more monotheistic feeling, and a Creator, either Hiranyagarbha or

---

[1] Dr Lorinser's attempt (*Die Bhagavadgītā*, ubersetzt und erlautert von Dr. F. Lorinser, 1869) to prove that the author of the *Gītā* borrowed many ideas from the Bible must be pronounced a failure. *Cf.* Garbe, 19, 83-85 ; Max Müller, *Natural Religion*, 97-100 ; Hopkins, *R. I.*, 429.

[2] On the religion of the *Rigveda* see Kaegi, 27-74; Hopkins, *R. I.*, Chaps. II-VI , Macdonell, 67-115 ; Bose, *H.C.*, I, 6-9 ; Dutt, *C.A.I.*, Vol. I, Chap. V , Monier-Williams, Chap. I.

[3] Hopkins, *R.I.*, 141 ; Macdonell, 385 ; Garbe, 1-2 ; Kaegi, 87.

[4] *E.g.*, X, 90.   [5] X, 81 ; 82; 121.

Visvakarman, is described. In others[1] the strain of thought is agnostic.

B. With the collection of the hymns of the *Rigveda* we pass into a new and very different period, the literature of which is altogether priestly. To this age belong the two great sacerdotal manuals, the *Sāmaveda*[2] or Chant-book, and the *Yajurveda*[1] or Sacrifice-book, and those extraordinary collections of priestly learning, mythology and mysticism, the Brāhmanas[3] These books introduce us to changed times and changed men, to new places and a new range of ideas. The fresh poetry of the youth of India has given place to the most prosaic and uninteresting disquisitions in the whole world.[5] The home of this literature is the great holy land of Brahman culture, stretching from the Sutlej on the West to the junction of the Jumna and the Ganges at Prayāga[6] In this period the doctrine of the transmigration of the soul first appears.[7]

C. The Aranyakas[8] and Upanishads[9] place before us a further development of Indian religion. Reflection led to the perception of the great truth, that the kernel of religion is not the ritual act but the heart of piety behind it. Many a man who had found the endless formulæ and the showy ceremonial of the sacrifice a serious hindrance to real religion, sought refuge from the noise and distraction of the popular cult in the lonely silence of forest or desert. To run over the sacrifice in one's own mind, they reasoned, was as acceptable to the gods as to kill the horse or to pour the ghee upon the altar fire. But they soon reached the further position, that for the man who has attained TRUE KNOWLEDGE sacrifice is altogether unnecessary. For knowledge of the world-soul emancipates a man from the chain of births and

---

[1] X, 129.   [2] Kaegi, 3, Macdonell, 171-174.
[3] Kaegi, 4; Macdonell, 174-185.
[4] Kaegi, 5, Macdonell, 202 ff. ; Muller, *A.S.L.,* Chap. II, Bose, *H.C.,* I, 9-12.
[5] Muller, *A.S.L.,* 389.   [6] Hopkins, *R.I.,* 177.
[7] Gough, Chap. I ; Garbe, 2-7 ; Macdonell, 223 ; Hopkins, *R.I.,* 204.
[8] Muller, *A.S.L.,* 313 ff. ; Macdonell, 204 ; Kaegi, 5.
[9] Muller, *A.S.L.,* 316 ff.; Macdonell, 218 ff. ; Kaegi, 5 ; Bose, *H.C.,* I, 12-19.

deaths and leads to true felicity. The main purpose, thus, of the Upanishads, is to expound the nature of the world-soul. Their teaching is by no means uniform. Not only do the separate treatises differ the one from the other ; contradictory ideas are frequently to be met with in the same book. They all tend to idealistic monism ; they all agree in identifying the soul of man with the world-soul ; but on the questions, whether the latter is personal or impersonal, how spirit and matter are related, and how the human soul will join the divine soul after death, there is no unanimity.[1]

There is thus no speculative system to be drawn from these books. Those of their ideas that are held with settled, serious conviction, are taught rather dogmatically than philosophically ; and, on the other hand, where there is freedom of thought, there is rather a groping after the truth than any definite train of illumi-native reasoning. Yet this occasional, conversational, unconven-tional character gives these simple and sincere treatises their greatest charm, and fits them for that devotional use to which so many generations of pious readers have put them. To this early period there belong only the first great group of prose Upani-shads, the *Brihadāranyaka*, *Chāndogya*, *Taittirīya*, *Aitareya*, *Kaushītaki* and parts of the *Kena* [2]

D. In bold contrast to this unsystematic meditation on the Eternal Spirit there stands out the severe, clear-cut, scientific system of Kapila,[3] the first Indian thinker who dared to trust the unaided human mind. Buddhist tradition recognizes that he pre-ceded Buddha, and connects him with Kapila-vastu, the birth-place of Buddha, the site of which was discovered as recently as December 1896[4] He drew a sharp distinction between matter and spirit and declared both to be eternal, without beginning and without end. The material universe develops in accordance

---

[1] For the teaching of the Upanishads *see* Gough , Hopkins, *R. I.*, Chap. X , Garbe, 7-10.

[2] *See* Deussen on each of these Upanishads, especially p. 264 ; and *Cf.* Macdonell, 226

[3] Garbe, 10 ; Macdonell, 390, 393.

[4] Fuhrer, *Monograph on Buddha Sakyamuni's Birthplace*, Arch. Surv. of India, Vol. XXVI, Allahabad, 1897 ; Macdonell, 13.

with certain laws out of primeval matter, *prakriti*. Spirit, on the other hand, exists as an indefinite number of individual souls, each eternal. There is no supreme divine spirit. The value of this system lies chiefly in its severely logical method, which demands that all reasoning shall proceed from the known elements of experience. It has exercised a very great influence on Indian thought, partly by its method, but still more perhaps through its cardinal ideas, the eternity of matter, the eternity of individual souls, the three *gunas*, the great cosmic periods, and *kaivalya*, i. e, the attainment of salvation through the separation of the soul from matter. This great system is known by the name Sānkhya, *i. e.*, enumeration, seemingly on account of the numbering of the twenty-five *tattvas*, or principles, which it sets forth.[1]

Such is the *Sānkhya* system; but it would be dangerous to affirm that the whole came from Kapila; for no treatise written by him has come down. The earliest systematic manual of the philosophy extant to-day is the *Sānkhya-Kārikā* of Isvara-Krishna, which dates from the early Christian centuries[2]

E. Shortly after the Sānkhya system, and in close dependence upon it, there appeared Buddhism and Jainism; but as these great religions exercised no very definite influence on the main stream of Indian thought for several centuries, we shall not linger over them.

F. We notice next the second great group of Upanishads, the *Katha, Isā, Svetāsvatara, Mundaka, Mahānārāyana*,[3] which are all written in verse. That this group is later than the great prose Upanishads is abundantly clear from the changed form as well as from the more developed matter. "As contrasted with the five above-mentioned Upanishads with their awkward Brāhmana style and their allegorical interpretations of the ritual, the *Katha Upanishad* belongs to a very different period, a time in which men began to coin the gold of Upanishad thought into separate metrical aphorisms, and to arrange them together in a more or less loose connection."[4] Further signs of their belonging

---

[1] For the Sānkhya system, *see* Garbe, 10, 11, 29, 36, 45; Macdonell, 390-395; Dutt, *C. A. I.*, Vol. I, pp. 276 ff.　　　[2] Macdonell, 393.

[3] Macdonell, 226; Deussen, 261, 523, 288, 544, 241.　　[4] Deussen, 264.

to another stage of thought are their references, more or less clear, to the Sānkhya and Yoga philosophies,[1] and their tendency to adopt the doctrine of Grace,[2] *i.e.*, that salvation is not a fruit of true knowledge, but a gift of God. The idea of *Bhakti*, which became afterwards so popular, appears in this group of Upanishads only once.[3] Here also for the first time in Sanskrit literature the word *Sānkhya* occurs as the name of a system.[4]

But while these five metrical treatises are clearly later than the prose Upanishads, scholars are not agreed on the question of their relation to the great systems. Some[5] hold that the *Katha* is earlier, others[6] that it is later, than Buddhism ; Weber[7] believes that the *Svetāsvatara*, *Mundaka*, and *Mahānārāyana* depend not only on Kapila's system, but also on the *Yoga Sūtras* of Patanjali (see below), while others[8] believe that in these Upanishads we have scattered pieces of teaching which were later systematized. But whatever be the truth on these points, it is clear that these five are posterior to the first group, that their relative age is *Katha*, *Isā*, *Svetāsvatara*, *Mundaka* and *Mahānārāyana*,[9] and that this last belongs to quite a late date.[10] Along with these verse Upanishads we may take three prose works, which are manifestly still later,[11] the *Prasna*, *Maitrāyanīya* and *Māndūkya*.

G. Several centuries after the Sānkhya there appeared the Yoga philosophy, the text-book of which is the *Yoga Sūtras*. According to Indian tradition the founder of the school and the author of the Sūtras was Patanjali,[12] the well-known scholar who wrote the *Mahābhāshya* on Pānini's grammar. He accepts the metaphysics of the Sānkhya system, but postulates the existence of a personal god, and urges the value of Yoga practices for the attainment of *Kaiyalya*, that isolation of the soul from matter,

---

[1] *Katha*, 3,10-13; 6,6 ; 6, 7-11 ; 6, 14-18 ; *Svet.* passim ; *Mundaka*, 2, 1, 1-3 ; *Mahānā*, 63, 21. *Cf.* Deussen, *ad loca.*

[2] *Katha*, 2, 23 ; *Svet.* 3, 20 ; *Mundaka*, 3, 2-3. *Cf.* Hopkins, *R.I.*, 238.

[3] *Svet.* 6, 23.   [4] *Svet.* 6, 13.

[5] Muller, *Anthrop. Rel.*, 345 ; Oldenberg, *Budda*, 56.

[6] Weber, *Sits. Berli. Ak. 1890*, p. 930.   [7] *I. L*, 159.

[8] Deussen, 291, 308.   [9] Deussen, *ad loca*, Macdonell, 226.

[10] Deussen, 242.   [11] Deussen, *ad loca ;* Macdonell, 226.

[12] Garbe, 14 ; Macdonell, 396 ; Hopkins, *R. I.*, 495.

which, according to Kapila, is true salvation. Thus not one of the three main elements of his system is original; for Yoga practices have existed from a very early date in India. Yet his system is sufficiently marked off from others, first by his combination of Yoga practices with Sānkhya principles and a theistic theology, and, secondly, by his systematic treatment of Yoga methods.[1]

H. Later still than the Yoga philosophy is the systematic statement of the Vedānta point of view by Bādarāyana in his Sūtras, which are known either as *Brahma-sūtras, Sārīraka-sūtras* or *Vedānta-sūtras.*[2]

I. We next notice the latest development of Upanishad teaching, namely, that found in the Upanishads of the *Atharva-veda.* With the exception of three, namely, the *Mundaka, Prasna* and *Māndūkya* Upanishads, which we have already noticed, they are all very late.[3] They fall into four great groups, according as they teach (*a*) pure Vedantism, (*b*) Yoga practices, (*c*) the life of the Sannyāsin, or (*d*) Sectarianism.[4] For our purpose the last of the four is of the most importance. "These sectarian treatises interpret the popular gods Siva (under various names, such as Isāna, Mahesvara, Mahādeva) and Vishnu (as Nārāyana and Nrishinha) as personifications of the Atman. The different Avatārs of Vishnu are here regarded as human manifestations of the Atman."[5] Let readers note that the doctrine of Avatārs is quite unknown in the Vedas, the Brāhmanas, the early Upanishads and the Sūtras.[6] We may also note that in groups (*a*) and (*b*) we find what is not found in earlier Upanishads, namely, the phrase *Sānkhya-Yoga* used as the name of a system[7] Here also the doctrines of Grace and *Bhakti*, the beginnings of which we found in the verse Upanishads, are regularly taught.

---

[1] For the Yoga system, *see* Garbe, 14-15; Macdonell, 396-399 : Dutt, *C. A. I.,* Vol. I, pp. 285 ff.

[2] Garbe, 16-18; Macdonell, 400-402.

[3] Deussen, 4; Macdonell, 238; Dutt, *C. A. I.,* Vol. I, 119; Garbe, 69.

[4] Deussen, 541-543; Macdonell, 238-239.

[5] Macdonell, 239. *Cf.* Deussen, 543, Weber, *I. L.,* 153 ff.

[6] Bose, *H.C.,* Vol. I, 4.

[7] *Garbha,* 4, *Prānāgnihotra,* 1; *Sūlika,* passim.

J. The last development that we need mention is the teaching of the *Mahābhārata* and *Manu.* We take them together, not only because each of them is the final product of long centuries of growth and compilation, but because they are so closely related to each other in origin, that it is hardly possible to take them separately.[1] In the first book of the *Mahābhārata* we are told that the poem originally consisted of only 8,800 *slokas*, and that at a later date the number was 24,000. The complete work now contains over 100,000 *slokas*.[2] We need not here enquire when the simple heroic lays were composed, which lie at the basis of the great composition as it has come down to us ; nor need we stay to decide at what period it finally reached its present labyrinthine structure and immense dimensions.[3] It is sufficient for our purpose to notice that scientific investigations have laid bare four stages in the formation of the Epic :—(*a*) early heroic songs, strung together into some kind of unity : this is the stage recognised in Book I, when the poem had only 8,800 *slokas*, and is in all probability the point at which it is referred to by Asvalāyana ; (*b*) a Mahābhārata story with Pandu heroes, and Krishna as a demi-god . this is the form in which it had 24,000 *slokas*, and is the stage of the poem referred to by Pānini ; (*c*) the Epic re-cast, with Krishna as All-god, and a great deal of didactic matter added , (*d*) later interpolations.[4] Scholars are able to fix, within certain limits, the dates of these various stages. We need not attempt to be so precise   for us it is enough that *the representation of Krishna as the Atman belongs to the third stage of the growth of the Epic.* Parallel with this third stage is the final redaction of *Manu.*[5] The philosophic standpoint of these two great works is practically the same, being now the *Sānkhya-Yoga,* now a mixture of Sānkhya, Yoga and Vedantic elements.[6]

---

[1] Macdonell, 428 ; Hopkins, *G.E.I.*, 18-23.   [2] Macdonell, 282-4.

[3] *See* Hopkins, *G. E. I.*, Chap. VI ; *R.I.*, 350 ; Macdonell, 285-288.

[4] Hopkins, *G. F. I.*, 397-398 ; Macdonell, 283-286. Bunkim Chundra recognizes the second, third and fourth of these stages . see *Krishnacharitra,* Chap. XI.

[5] *The Ordinances of Manu,* Burnell and Hopkins, pp. XIX-XXVIII, Macdonell, 428.

[6] Hopkins, *G. E. I.*, Chap. III ; *R. I.* 266.

But the main thing to notice is that in these books we are
already in modern Hinduism. Turning from the Vedas to them
we find ourselves in an altogether new world. There are many
new gods ; most of the old divinities have fallen to subordinate
places   New customs, new names and ideas are found everywhere.
The language too has changed : new words, new expressions and
new forms occur in plenty ; old words occur in new senses ,
while many others have disappeared.[1]

*   *   *   *   *

Let us now turn to the *Gītā.*   What is its place in this long
succession ?   Clearly it is posterior, not only to our first, but also
to our second group of Upanishads. For it echoes the *Katha,*
the *Svetāsvatara,* and several of the others repeatedly ;[2] its
versification is decidedly later in character :[3] the doctrines of
Grace and of *Bhakti,* which are found in these Upanishads only
in germ, are fully developed in the *Gītā ;*[4] while the whole theory
of Krishna is a fresh growth.

The *Gītā* may also be shewn to belong to the same age as the
Atharvan Upanishads. It has in common with them (*a*) the
identification of Krishna and Vishnu with the *Atman,* (*b*) the
doctrine of Avatārs,[5] (*c*) the doctrines of Grace and *Bhakti,* (*d*)
the Sānkhya-Yoga.

But we may go further, and show that the *Gītā* is in its teaching, in general, parallel with the third stage of the *Mahābhārata*
and with *Manu.*   For while the usual philosophic standpoint in the
Song is Sānkhya-Yoga, there are frequent lapses to the Vedānta ;
and there is an evident effort here and there to combine all three.[6]
This is precisely the position of *Manu* and the Epic, as we have
seen.   Note that in the *Gītā* the Yoga philosophy is already old,
so old that it has fallen into decay, and requires to be resusci-
tated[7]   The Sānkhya is not a loose group of ideas, but a formed
system, as appears from the phrases *Sānkhya-Kritānta*[8] and
Guna-sankhyāna.[9]   Kapila, its author, is so far in the past that he

[1] Hopkins, *R. I.,* Chaps. XIV and XV ; Bose, *H. C.,* Vol. I, 3.
[2] *See* Telang's translation throughout, and *cf.* Hopkins, *G. E I.,* 28-46 ;
Amalnerkar, 4-5.   [3] Telang, 15.   [4] *Cf.* Hopkins, *R. I.,* 429.
[5] *G.,* IV, 8.   [6] Hopkins, *R. I.,* 399.   [7] *G.,* IV, 1-3.
[8] *G.,* XVIII, 13. [9] *G.,* XVIII, 10.

is canonized as the chief of the *Siddhas*.[1] There are many minor points which the *Gītā* holds in common with the *Mahābhārata*, and which are not found earlier. The latter half of the tenth chapter is full of Epic mythology. There Skanda is the great warrior-god,[2] as in the *Mahābhārata*;[3] there too we find the horse Uccaih-sravas,[4] the elephant Airāvata,[5] the snake Vāsuki,[6] the fish Makara.[7] *Nirvāna* is used in the *Gītā*[8] for 'highest bliss,' 'Brahmic bliss,' precisely as in the Epic.[9] In the *Mahābhārata* Bhīshma, after receiving his mortal wound, has to wait for the *Uttarāyana* (the northward journey of the sun), *i. e.*, he has to wait until the sun passes the southern solstice, before he can die in safety.[10] In the *Gītā* we find a similar idea : only those devotees who die during the *Uttarāyana* go to Brahman ; those who die during the *Dakshināyana* return to earth.[11] This dogma is not found in the early Upanishads nor yet in the Sūtras.[12]

A study of the language of the *Gītā*[13] leads to the same conclusion. A portion of its vocabulary is the same as that of the first group of Upanishads ; a larger portion coincides with our second group ; a still larger coincides with the diction of the Atharvan group , and finally, much that is found in no Upanishad is characteristic of the Epic.

We need not attempt to fix the date[14] of the poem, for that is not only impossible as yet, but is quite unnecessary for our purpose.

---

[1] *G*, X, 26. This is a noticeable point , for Kapila is the only founder of a philosophical system known to the Epic ; he alone is authoritative in all philosophical matters. *See* Hopkins, *G. E. I.*, 97.

[2] *G.*, X, 24.   [3] *See* Hopkins, *R. I.*, 414.   [4] *G.*, X, 27.

[5] *G.*, X, 27   [6] *G.*, X, 28.   [7] *G.*, X, 31.

[8] *G*, II, 72 ; V, 24 ; 25 ; 26 ; VI, 15.

[9] Hopkins, *G. E. I.*, 88 , *R. I.*, 427.   [10] *Mahābhārata*, Bhīshma Parvan.

[11] *G.*, VIII, 24-25.   [12] Amalnerkar, 13.

[13] See *Jacob's Concordance to the Principal Upanishads and Bhagavad-gītā*

[14] Mr. Justice Telang was inclined to put the date before the third century B.C., but his otherwise most judicious criticism is faulty in this that it does not take all the factors of the problem into consideration. Others, such as Müller, Weber, Davies and Lorinser, incline to a very late date, about the third century A.D. Most writers believe that the true date lies between these extremes. So Monier-Williams, Hopkins, Fraser and others. Prof. Amalnerkar's

What we wish to do is to show that the religious literature of India displays a long, regular, evolutionary process, that the *Gītā* belongs to the same period as the third stage of the *Mahābhārata*, and is itself clearly the result of all the preceding development.

*   *   *   *

Can we then accept the declaration of the poem itself, that it was uttered by Krishna on the battlefield of Kuiukshetra?— That necessarily depends upon the history and the chronology. At what point then in the historical development of the literature which we have been studying does the famous battle stand ?— According to all scholars the great war and the compilation of the *Vedas* both belong to the same period.[1]

The results of our study may, therefore, be tabulated as follows, with the proviso that the long process of the growth of the Epic cannot be fully represented :—

The Hymns of the Vedas.
Compilation of the Vedas....................KURUKSHETRA.
The Brāhmanas.
The prose Upanishads.
Kapila.
Buddhism and Jainism.
The verse Upanishads.
Patanjali.
Bādarāyana.
The Atharvan Upanishads.
The third stage of the Epic and *Manu* ....THE GITA.

---

pamphlet contains a number of most interesting points. His contention, that the phrase, *Brahmasūtrapadaih* (G. XIII, 4) refers to the *Vedānta Sūtras*, and that the *Gītā* is therefore the later work of the two, has been accepted by Max Muller (*S. S. I. P.*, 155), but Prof. Hopkins thinks the *Gītā* is earlier than the Sūtra (*R. I.*, 400). The theory which Prof. Hopkins holds, that the Divine Song was originally an Upanishad, and that it was redacted, first as a Vishuite poem, and then a second time in the interests of Krishnaism (*R. I.*, 389), would account, on the one hand, for the numerous inconsistencies in its teaching, and, on the other, for the very conflicting signs of date which it presents. For a criticism of Bunkim Chundra's views, *see* the Appendix.

[1] Dutt, *C. A. I.*, Vol. I, 9-11 ; Bunkim Ch. Chatterji, *Krishnacharitra*, 46 ; Macdonell, 174-175, 285 ; Hopkins, *R. I.*, 33, 177-179.

It has thus become perfectly clear that THE GITA CANNOT
HAVE BEEN UTTERED ON THE BATTLEFIELD OF KURUKSHETRA;
for it is the last member of a long series, the final product of a
clearly defined and elaborate process of development. To ascribe
the *Gītā* to the age of Kurukshetra is much the same as if one
were to ascribe the poetry of Tennyson to the age of Alfred the
Great. A thousand years intervene ; the thought and toil of a
millenium were needed to produce the great result.

Had Krishna uttered these doctrines on the famous battlefield,
we should inevitably have found references to them in the literature produced during the following centuries. But where in the
Brāhmanas do we find any of the leading ideas of the *Gītā ?*
Even if men had disbelieved Krishna, his claim to be God incarnate would at least have drawn out a protest ; but in no single
Brāhmana or early Upanishad is there the slightest hint of anything of the kind. So far from there being any corroboration of the
great myth in early literature, there is the clearest proof that it is
false. In the *Kāthaka* recension of the *Black Yajur Veda* king
Dhritarāshtra is mentioned as a well-known person[1] ; yet in the
whole literature of the Black Yajur there is no suggestion that
Krishna claimed divine honours. *The Satapatha Brāhmana,*
which is a product of the *Kuru-Panchāla* country,[2] contains the
names of a number of the heroes of the great war,[3] but never refers
to Krishna as God incarnate ; while in the *Chāndogya Upanishad,*[4]
which belongs to the same district,[5] he is spoken of merely as a
man : he is mentioned as a pupil of Ghora Angirasa and is called
Krishna Devakiputra.[6] Nay, even in the earliest part of the *Mahābhārata* itself Krishna is only a great chief, and not a deity at all.[7]

---

[1] Macdonell, 285 ; Weber, *I. L.*, 90.

[2] *S. B. E.*, Vol. XII, pp. XLI-XLII, Macdonell, 213.

[3] *S. B. E.*,Vol. XIV, Index. *Cf.* Weber, *I. L.*, 186, *Krishnacharitra*, 31.

[4] 3, 17, 6. *See* Dutt, *C. A. I.*, Vol. I, 189, Weber, *I. L.*, 71 , Bose,
H. C., Vol I, 26 ; Hopkins, *R. I.*, 465.

[5] Weber, *I. L.*, 70.

[6] Whether Krishna Angirasa in the *Kaushītaki Brāhmana* be the same
person as Krishna Devakiputra, or not, we cannot tell.

[7] Dutt, *C. A. I.*, Vol. I, 127 ; Bose, *H. C.*, Vol. I, 33-34 ; Hopkins, *R. I.*,
403 ; Monier-Williams, 112,

Finally, the references to Pandu heroes and to the worship of Krishna and Arjuna in Pāṇini,[1] would lead to the conclusion that in Pāṇini's day Krishna was not regarded as the supreme God, but as one among many ;[2] and this cautious inference is corroborated by the fact that the *Mahābhāshya* itself does not recognize him as the incarnation of Brahma, but as a hero and demi-god[3] *Thus the whole of the Vedic literature, and the whole of the Sūtra literature, are destitute of a single reference to Krishna as the incarnation of the Supreme.* There is only one conclusion to be drawn from this overwhelming mass of evidence.[4]

It is strange that educated Hindus should have clung so long to the idea that the *Gītā* is a real utterance of Krishna. The very fact that the poem has always been regarded, not as *Sruti,* but simply as *Smriti,* should have been enough to suggest the truth. A piece of genuine divine teaching, uttered in such circumstances, and before the composition of the earliest Upanishads, would have inevitably found a place among the most authoritative scriptures of the faith. The fact of its having been always regarded as *Smriti* is sufficient proof by itself that the book does not belong to the Vedic age at all. Another consideration ought also by itself to have been sufficient to save Hindus from such a grave error, namely, this, that *no great religious advance or upheaval followed the time when Krishna is supposed to have lived and taught.* Contrast the mighty revolutions that followed the work of Buddha, of Christ and of Mahommed ; and the emptiness of the Krishna claim will become at once apparent.

Again, the subject of all the early Upanishads is the nature of the Supreme Spirit, whether called the *Atman* or *Brahma.* If

---

[1] The reference to Krishna and Arjuna runs *Vāsudevārjunābhyām vun* (IV, 3, 98), words which put the two on one level.

[2] Hopkins, *G E. I* , 390-395.　　[3] Hopkins, *G. E. I.,* 395.

[4] We need not stay to ask whether the *Srimadbhāgavat* and other Purānas can be trusted as evidence for the life of Krishna ; for all scholars agree that, while ancient Puranas existed, all those that have come down to us reflect *a later stage of Hinduism than that of the Mahābhārata ,* and that, while they contain much that is old scattered up and down their pages, the oldest fragments are of the same general date as the *Mahābhārata* and *Manu.* Hopkins, *R. I.,* 434-445 ; Macdonell, 299-302 ; Dutt, *C. A. I.,* I, 19 ; II, 211 ; Muller, *A. S. L.,* 61 ; Kaegi, 8, 105 ; *Krishnacharitra,* Chaps. XIV-XVI.

on the field of Kurukshetra, Krishna had claimed to be the
Supreme, as the *Gītā* says he did, can any one believe that the
claim could have been passed unnoticed in the Upanishads?
Krishna is mentioned in the *Chāndogya;* Brahma is the subject
of the *Chāndogya:* yet there is not the slightest hint anywhere
that Brahma has been incarnated, far less that Krishna is Brahma.
Such evidence is surely irresistible.

One reason why the truth about this myth has been so long
in finding its way into the minds of educated Hindus is undoubtedly to be found in the wretchedly inadequate way in which
Sanskrit literature is taught in the Universities of India. In
Calcutta at least most men who take Sanskrit as one of their sub-
jects for the B. A. Degree get through their examination without
having the slightest knowledge of the history of the literature.[1]
For some curious results of this very deficient training, see the
Appendix.

With Krishna, all the other so-called Avatārs vanish ; for they
rest on foundations still more flimsy and fanciful. They merely
serve as signal proofs of the tendency inherent in the Hindu mind
to believe in incarnations and to see such around them. This
tendency was already living and creative long before the Christian
era, and it has kept its vitality down to the present day ; for
though Chaitanya, the sixteenth-century reformer, is the most
noteworthy of those who within recent times have been counted
Avatārs, he is by no means the last : the late Ramkrishna Param-
hamsa was regarded as such,[2] and some of her admirers claim
the same honour for Mrs. Annie Besant [3] Further, this making
of Avatārs is but one aspect of that passion for deifying men which
has characterized Hinduism from first to last,[4] a passion which
has set many a modern Englishman among the gods. Even such
a whole-hearted Christian as John Nicholson did not escape.[5]

---

[1] The study of Prof. Macdonell's excellent manual ought surely now to
be made part of any Sanskrit course prescribed for a University degree in
India.

[2] Bose, *H. C.*, Vol. I, 5.   [3] *The Student's Chronicle*, May 1903, p. 6.

[4] For some amusing instances *see* Hopkins, *R. I.*, 522, note, and *cf.*
Monier-Williams, Chap. X.

[5] Monier-Williams, 260.

The story, then, that Krishna uttered the Song on the battlefield, is a pious imagination. All scholars hold the war to be
historical ; Krishna's name can be traced in the literature from the
Upanishads downwards ; it is possible, or even probable, that he
was a Kshattriya prince[1] who fought in the war , but *the assertion
that on the field he claimed to be the supreme being, is absolutely
negatived by all the early history and literature of India.*

     *   *   *

How then are we to account for the *Gītā?* Whence came
its power and its beauty? and how did it reach the form it has ?—
We must recognise the action of three factors in the formation of
the Song, the philosophy, the worship of Krishna, and the author.
We have already traced in outline the genesis of the philosophy ;
there remain the cult and the author.

All our scholars recognize that Krishna-worship has existed in
India since the fourth century B. C. at least ; for there can be no
doubt that, when Megasthenes says that Herakles was worshipped
in Methora and Kleisobora,[2] he means that Krishna was worshipped in Mathura and Krishnapur. How much further back the
cult goes we have no means of learning. Nor does it really
matter for our purpose. The important thing to realize is the
existence of this worship of Krishna, before his identification with
Vishnu[3] and final exaltation to the place of the supreme pan-
theistic divinity.

The author of the *Gītā* was clearly a man of wide and deep
culture. He had filled his mind with the best religious philosophy
of his country. He was catholic rather than critical, more inclined to piece things together than to worry over the differences

---

[1] Garbe, 85 , Monier-Williams, 98, 112, note.

[2] McCrindle, *Ancient India*, 201. *Cf.* Hopkins, *R. I.*, 459; Macdonell, 411 , Dutt, *C. A. I.*, Vol. I, 219 ; Garbe, 19, 83.

[3] That it was only at a very late date that this identification took place is
evident from the fact that it is not once mentioned in the early literature.
Even in two of the Vishnu Upanishads of the Atharva Veda, the *Atmabodha,*
and the *Nārāyana,* Krishna is referred to as a mere man. Apart from the
Gītā and the *Mahābhārata,* the earliest reference to him as God incarnate
is in the *Gopālatāpanīyopanishad.* See Weber, *I. L.,* 169 ; and *cf.* Garbe,
18-19, 85 ; Bose, *H. C.*, Vol. I, 25-26 ; Dutt, *C. A. I.*, Vol. II, 191.

between them. Each of the philosophic systems appealed to his sympathetic mind · he was more impressed with the value of each than with the distinctions between them. But his was not only a cultured but a most reverent mind. He was as fully in sympathy with Krishna-worship as with the philosophy of the Atman. Indeed, it was the union of these qualities in him that fitted him to produce the noblest and purest expression of modern Hinduism. For Hinduism is just the marriage of ancient Brāhmanical thought and law with the popular cults. But without his splendid literary gifts the miracle would not have been possible. The beauty, precision and power of the diction of the poem, and its dignity of thought, rising now and then to sublimity, reveal but one aspect of his masterly literary ability. Much of the success of the poem arises from his genuine appreciation of the early heroic poems, which he heard recited around him, and from his consequent decision to make his own Song, in one sense at least, a heroic poem. Lastly, there is the shaping spirit of imagination, without which no man can be a real poet. With him this power was introspective rather than dramatic. No poet with any genuine dramatic faculty would have dreamed of representing a warrior as entering on a long philosophic discussion on the field of battle at the very moment when the armies stood ready to clash On the other hand, what marvellous insight is displayed in his representation of Krishna ! Who else could have imagined with such success how an incarnate god would speak of himself? Nor must we pass on without noticing that, though the situation in which the Song is supposed to have been produced is an impossible one, yet for the author's purpose it is most admirably conceived : how otherwise could the main thought of the book—*philosophic calm leading to disinterested action*— have been so vividly impressed on the imagination ?

This author, then, formed the idea of combining the loftiest philosophy of his country with the worship of Krishna. He would intertwine the speculative thought that satisfied the intellect with the fervid devotion which even the uncultured felt for a god who was believed to have walked the earth. Philosophy would thus come nearer religion, while religion would be placed on far surer intellectual ground. His tastes led him to connect his work with the romantic poems of the day; his genius suggested the situation, a dialogue between a noble knight and the incarnate divinity; his catholicity taught him to interweave the Sānkhya with the Yoga and both with the Vedānta; and as we have seen, his penetrative imagination was equal to the creation of the subjective consciousness of a god-man.

We can now answer the question which stands at the head of this chapter, What is the *Bhagavadgītā?* It consists of two distinct elements, one old, one original. The philosophy is old; for it is only a very imperfect combination [1] of what is taught in earlier books. The original element is the teaching put into Krishna's mouth about his own person and the relation in which he stands to his own worshippers and to others. Of this part of the teaching of the *Gītā* we here give a brief analysis:—

> Krishna is first of all the source of the visible world. All
> comes from him,[2] all rests in him.[3] At the end of a Kalpa
> everything returns to him,[4] and is again reproduced.[5]
> He pervades all things,[6] and again, in another sense,
> he is all that is best and most beautiful in nature and
> in man.[7] But while Krishna is thus the supreme
> power in the universe,[8] he is altogether without personal
> interest in the activity therein displayed:[9] he sits un-
> concerned,[10] always engaged in action,[11] yet controlling
> his own nature,[12] and therefore never becoming bound

---

[1] For the inconsistencies of the *Gītā*, see Telang, p. 11; Hopkins, *R. I.*, 399, 399-400.

[2] VII, 6; 10, IX, 8; 10; 13; XIV, 3.   [3] VII, 7; IX, 5.

[4] IX, 7.   [5] IX, 7.   [6] IX, 4.   [7] VII, 8-11; X, 20-38.

[8] IX, 10; 17-18.   [9] IV, 14.   [10] IX, 9.   [11] III, 22-24.

[12] This is Telang's translation of two very difficult, yet very instructive phrases In the *Gītā* the word *prakriti* is used, first for the primeval matter of the Sānkhya system (III, 27; 29; IX, 8, 10, 12; XIII, 19, 20, 23, 29), and secondly for the primeval matter of personal character, each man's natural disposition (III, 33, VII, 20; XI, 51; XVIII, 59). There is then a third class of passages in which the word is used in the Sānkhyan sense, but, *by the addition of a personal pronoun, prakriti* is made to belong to Krishna personally (VII, 4, 5; IX, 7, 13). Here we have one of the devices our author employed to give the great old phrases a vivid personal colouring. Now such a phrase as "my prakriti" is already ambiguous; so we are not

2

by the results of his action.[1] This conception of the
Supreme, as at once the centre of all activity and yet
completely detached, enables the author, on the one
hand, to soften the seemingly hopeless contradiction
involved in identifying the king, warrior and demon-
slayer, Krishna, with the passionless, characterless
Atman[2] of the Upanishads, and, on the other to
hold up Krishna as the supreme example of Action
Yoga.

We now turn to Krishna's relation to his worshippers.
Knowledge is good ,[3] mental concentration is better ;[4]
disinterested action is better than either ;[5] but the
supreme wisdom is faith in Krishna and boundless
devotion to him.[6] Such is the teaching of the *Gītā*.
The worst epithets are kept for those who fail to
recognise him as the Supreme, who disregard him,
carp at him, hate him.[7] To those who resort to
Krishna,[8] who place faith in him,[9] who shower on
him their love, devotion and worship,[10] who rest on
him,[11] think of him[12] and remember him[13] at all times,—
to them are promised forgiveness,[14] release from the

---

surprised to meet with two passages, in which it is impossible to tell whether
the meaning is metaphysical or ethical (IV, 6 , IX, 8). Probably the author
intended to suggest both meanings. Most translators take the meaning to be
metaphysical, but Telang may be right in taking it as ethical Krishna is
regarded as the ideal of Action Yoga. For a similar use of the personal
pronoun compare *sarvakarmāni mayi sannyasya* (XVIII, 57) with *sarvakarmāni sannyasya* of the *Paramahansopanishad*. Pages 706, 708 and 709 of
Jacob's *Concordance to the Principal Upanishads and Bhagavadgītā* are peculiarly instructive in this connection.

[1] IV, 14 ; IX, 9.   [2] X, 12, 20.
[3] III, 3 ; IV, 36-38 ; XII, 12.   [4] XII, 12 ; XIII, 24.
[5] II, 47-53 ; III, 7, 30 , IV, 14-23 ; V, 2 ; VI, 1, XII, 12 , XVIII,
1-11.
[6] VII, 13-14 ; XII, 20.   [7] VII, 15 ; IX, 11-12 ; XVI, 6-20.
[8] II, 61, VII, 14 ; XII, 6 ; XVIII, 57.   [9] XII, 2.
[10] VI, 14, 31 ; IX, 13-14, 22, 30, 34 ; X, 8-10, XII, 2, 6-7, 14.
[11] IV, 10 ; VII, 1, 29 ; IX, 32.   [12] VI, 14 ; X, 9, XVIII, 57-58.
[13] VIII, 5, 7, 14.   [14] X, 3 ; XVIII, 66.

bonds of action,[1] attainment of tranquillity,[2] true knowledge[3] and final bliss[4] in Krishna.[5]

Since all the gods come from Krishna,[6] and since he is in the last resort the sole reality,[7] worship offered to other gods is in a sense offered to him.[8] He accepts it and rewards it [9] This is in accordance with his indifference to men : to him no one is hateful, no one dear.[10] Yet the highest blessings fall only to those who recognize him directly.[11]

Clearly our author formed his conception of the man-god with great skill, and fitted it into his general scheme with all the care and precision he was capable of. On this elaboration of the self-consciousness of Krishna he concentrated all his intellectual and imaginative powers. And with what unequalled success ! Could any greater compliment be paid an author than to have sixty generations of cultured readers take the creation of his mind for a transcript from history?

*   *   *   *   *

The masses of evidence we have marshalled to prove that Krishna never claimed to be God, may be briefly summarised as follows :—

1. The situation in which the *Gītā* is said to have been uttered at once strikes the historical student as suspicious : one can scarcely believe that there was ever a battle in which such a thing could have taken place ; and, on the other hand, it makes such an excellent background to the theory of Action Yoga, that one cannot help believing that it was invented for the very purpose. Further investigation leads to the following results :—

2. The characteristic religious and philosophical ideas of the *Gītā* are not found in any books produced immediately after the age of Kurukshetra. If we start with the teaching of that

---

[1] IV, 14 ; IX, 28 ; XVIII, 49.   [2] V, 29 ; VI, 15 ; XVIII, 62.
[3] X, 11.   [4] VI, 15 , VIII, 15
[5] IV, 9 ; VII, 19 ; VIII, 5, 7, 15-16 ; IX, 25, 28, 32, 34 , XII, 8 ; XIII, 18 ; XIV, 2 ; XVIII, 55-56, 62, 65.
[6] X, 2.   [7] X, 1-3, 20.   [8] IX, 23,
[9] VII, 21-22.   [10] IX, 29.   [11] IX, 22 , X, 7-11.

age, we have to trace the stages o a long and clearly-marked development before we reach the ideas of the *Gītā*]

3 The diction of the *Gītā* is not the Vedic Sanskrit of the early *Brāhmanas* (which are the literature of the period following Kurukshetra), but belongs to a very much later stage of the language.

4. The fact that the *Gītā* is not *sruti*, but *smriti*, proves that it comes neither from Krishna, nor from the time of Kurukshetra.

5. Krishna Devakiputra is known in the later Vedic literature as a man, and in the Sūtra literature as a hero or demi-god, but never as the supreme being.

6. The fact that there is not a single reference in the whole of the Vedic literature, nor yet in the Sūtra literature, to Krishna as the incarnation of Brahma, makes it impossible for us to believe that at the battle of Kurukshetra he claimed to be such.

7. The fact that there was no revival or reformation of religion in the age of Kurukshetra proves that God was not incarnated then.

CHAPTER II.

PLATO'S JUST MAN.

WE must now leave the land of Bhārata and seek the shores of Greece.

In the fifth century, B C., Athens became the focus of Hellenic culture. Her achievements in the Persian wars had given her very distinctly the leadership of all the Greek states ; and the steady progress of her commerce brought her not only wealth but abundant intercourse with other cities So that in the latter half of the century we find the peculiar genius of Hellas displayed in Athens with unexampled vigour, variety and splendour. But space will not allow us even to outline the achievements of that incomparable age in the various provinces of human culture. We must confine our attention to philosophy.

The general advance of intelligence, education and culture in Greece produced the only result possible in communities whose religion was a traditional polytheism and whose morality rested merely on custom and proverbial wisdom · scepticism,, both religious and ethical, broke in like a flood. Tradition and custom could not withstand the corrosive influences of fresh thought fed by deepening experience and widening science. The Sophists were the exponents, but scarcely the creators, of this sceptical habit of thought. The philosophers had not done much to cause it, and they could do as little to cure it. Their theories dealt with nature rather than man, and stood in no clear relation to the problems that agitated every thinking mind.

It was at Athens that this sceptical spirit showed itself most conspicuously, now in the lectures of the chief Sophists of Hellas, naturally drawn to the centre of intellectual ferment, now in the stately tragedies of her Dionysiac festivals, now in the *fin-de-siècle* conversation of her gilded youth. The timid, the old-fashioned, the conservative scolded and sputtered and threatened, blaming individuals instead of the time spirit, but had no healing word to utter.[1]

From the very centre of the disturbance came the new spirit of order and restoration . Socrates, the Athenian, saved Greece. The older philosophers had discussed nature ; he turned all his attention to practical human life. Like the Sophists, he trusted human reason ; but unlike them, he aimed not at a display of intellectual dexterity but at reaching the actual basis of human morality, society and politics. Human conduct was the sole subject of his thought and his conversation. Hence the definite, practical value of his influence : his teaching stood in the closest possible relation to life and to the problems of the time. On the other hand, he began with introspection ; self-knowledge was what he demanded of every disciple. Hence the inexhaustible significance of his work for philosophy. He gave no set lessons to his pupils, delivered no lectures, wrote no books. He spent his whole time in conversation with individuals, proceeding always by question and answer, thus compelling his companion to think for himself. His extraordinary intellectual skill and the loftiness and simplicity of his character drew all the best intellects of Athens around him. But what gives him his unchallenged supremacy in the history of Greek thought is the fact, that in his hands the sceptical thought, which had caused such dismay everywhere, proved to be the very means of revealing the great realities which men had feared for [2]

In 399 B. C., when he was an old man of seventy years of age, a number of his fellow-citizens brought a criminal case against him, charging him with corrupting the youth of Athens and with impiety. He was tried, found guilty and sentenced to death. A month later he drank the hemlock—such was the Athenian mode of execution—surrounded by his friends.[3]

---

[1] Zeller, *Socrates,* Chaps. I and II.

[2] Zeller, *Socrates,* Chaps. III to IX ; Bury, *History of Greece,* II, 140—146 ; Grote, *History of Greece,* Chap. LXVIII.

[3] Zeller, *Socrates,* Chap. X , Bury, *History of Greece,* II, 147.

How tragic! Athens, "the school of Hellas,"[1] kills her greatest teacher! Socrates, the father of ethical philosophy, the founder of the critical method, the ideal instructor, dies as an impious corruptor of the youth of Athens!

But Socrates was not merely the greatest teacher of his day. All subsequent Greek philosophy is filled with his spirit; indeed the leading schools of thought were founded by his pupils.[2] Consequently he is the fountain-head of all Western philosophy and science; for in both Greece was the school-mistress of Europe.

Among all the disciples, Plato best represents the master's spirit. The Megarians, the Cynics, the Cyrenaics, and, at a later date, the Stoics and the Epicureans, certainly carried on the work of Socrates, but they are deflections from the straight line: they are "imperfect schools," as Zeller calls them.[3] Plato is in the direct line of succession

He was about twenty years of age when he began to listen to Socrates. Eight years later came the death of the great teacher. Plato then left Athens and spent a number of years in travel and in study in different places. About 390 B C, however, he returned to the city and set up a philosophical school in a garden called Academia. For forty years thereafter he was the acknowledged leader of philosophic thought and teaching in Athens.[4] His influence since his death has rested chiefly on his Dialogues, one of the most perfect literary treasures in the Greek language. The form of these beautiful compositions still reflects the question-and-answer method of Plato's master; and the debt of the pupil is everywhere acknowledged; for in most of the Dialogues Socrates is the chief interlocutor.[5] Among the Dialogues the *Republic* is universally recognized as the most precious; for it shows us not only his literary art at its highest, but the thought of his matured mind: it represents Plato in his strength.[6]

---

[1] So called by Pericles, her greatest statesman. See *Thucydides*, II, 41.

[2] See Milton, *Paradise Regained*, IV, 272-280.

[3] *Socrates*, Part III.

[4] Mahaffy, *Greek Literature*, II, 160-162; Ritchie, *Plato*, Chap. I; Mayor, *Ancient Philosophy*, 41 ff.

[5] For the Dialogues *see* Ritchie's *Plato*, Chap. II.

[6] On the *Republic* see Mahaffy, *Greek Literature*, II, 195-201.

The subject of the *Republic* is "What is Justice?" It is thus the culmination of the ethical teaching of Socrates. Among the preliminary discussions in this book there occurs a very striking conversation between Glaucon and Socrates, in which the former gives two ideal portraits, one of a man consummately unjust, the other of a man altogether just. Here is the passage .—

"But in actually deciding between the lives of the two persons in question, we shall be enabled to arrive at a correct conclusion by contrasting together the thoroughly just and the thoroughly unjust man,—and only by so doing. Well then, how are we to contrast them? In this way. Let us make no deduction either from the injustice of the unjust, or from the justice of the just, but let us suppose each to be perfect in his own line of conduct. First of all then, the unjust man must act as skilful craftsmen do. For a first-rate pilot or physician perceives the difference between what is practicable and what is impracticable in his art, and while he attempts the former, he lets the latter alone; and, moreover, should he happen to make a false step, he is able to recover himself. In the same way, if we are to form a conception of a consummately unjust man, we must suppose that he makes no mistake in the prosecution of his unjust enterprises and that he escapes detection: but if he be found out, we must look upon him as a bungler; for it is the perfection of injustice to seem just without really being so. We must, therefore, grant to the perfectly unjust man, without any deduction, the most perfect injustice : and we must concede to him, that while committing the grossest acts of injustice, he has won himself the highest reputation for justice; and that should he make a false step, he is able to recover himself, partly by a talent for speaking with effect, in case he be called in question for any of his misdeeds, and partly because his courage and strength, and his command of friends and money, enable him to employ force with success, whenever force is required. Such being our unjust man, let us, in pursuance of the argument, place the just man by his side, a man of true simplicity and nobleness, resolved, as Æschylus says, not to seem, but to be, good. We must certainly take away the seeming; for if he be thought to be a just man, he will have honours and gifts on the strength of this reputation, so that it will be uncertain whether it is for justice's sake, or for the sake of the gifts and honours, that he is what he is. Yes; we must strip him bare of everything but justice, and make his whole case the reverse of the former. Without being guilty of one unjust act, let him have the worst reputation for injustice, so that his virtue may be thoroughly tested, and shewn to be proof against infamy and all its consequences ; and let him go on till the day of his death, stead-fast in his justice, but with a lifelong reputation for injustice ; in order that, having brought both the men to the utmost limits of justice and of injustice respectively, we may then give judgment as to which of the two is the happier."

"Good heavens ! my dear Glaucon, " said I, "how vigorously you work, scouring the two characters clean for our judgment, like a pair of statues."

"I do it as well as I can," he said. "And after describing the men as we have done, there will be no further difficulty, I imagine, in proceeding to sketch the kind of life which awaits them respectively. Let me there-fore describe it. And if the description be somewhat coarse, do not regard it as mine, Socrates, but as coming from those who commend in-justice above justice They will say that in such a situation the just man will be scourged, racked, fettered, will have his eyes burnt out, and at last, after suffering every kind of torture, will be crucified ; and thus learn that it is best to resolve, not to be, but to seem, just." [1]

The picture of the just man here is surely a very remarkable one. It is dramatically put into the mouth of Glaucon, and part of it is by him attributed to those who commend injustice ; but these are but literary forms ; the picture is Plato's own It is his ideal of the just man ; and the extraordinary thing is his belief, here stated so plainly, that a man whose heart is perfectly set on righteousness may be so completely misunderstood by those around him, as to be regarded by them as utterly unjust, and may in consequence be subjected to the extremest torture and the most shameful death.

No one can doubt that it was the death of his master that led Plato to perceive the great truth to which he here gives such energetic expression. The charges against Socrates were a com-plete inversion of the truth : his reverence was called impiety ; his brilliant work for the character of the youth of his day brought him the charge of baneful corruption. From his tragic end Plato learned that the good man who brings new truth is very likely to be completely misunderstood and to be classed with the worst wrong-doers.

---

[1] Plato, *Rep.*, II, 360 E—362 A, Davies and Vaughan's translation.

CHAPTER III.

THE SERVANT OF JEHOVAH.

THE history of Israel is unique in the annals of the nations. In size scarcely worthy of regard, in politics only for one brief reign of any serious account, with no special genius for art or war, for speculative thinking or scientific research, failing to keep even their racial unity in the day of their greatest strength, torn in pieces by every conqueror, deported out of their own land, and even after their return kept in subjection by other imperial races, finally stripped of their temple and sacred city by the Romans, and shattered into fragments, this feeble people has yet set its name high beside Greece and Rome, has given the world the only book which all the world reads,[1] and the religion which has produced Western civilization.

The one duty of which the best spirits in Israel were conscious throughout the history of the people was faithfulness to Jehovah. Indeed the whole consciousness of the race might be summed up in two phrases : *Jehovah is the God of Israel*, and, *Israel is the people of Jehovah*. War, government, philosophy, art might be for other peoples : Israel's one duty was to serve her God, religion the sole activity of her spirit.

---

[1] The Bible, complete or in part, is printed and published to-day in 454 languages and dialects. The number of Bibles, New Testaments and portions sold by the various Bible Societies of Europe and America, in lands outside Europe, amounted in 1901 to 3,286,834. (*Centennial Survey of Foreign Missions* by the Rev. James S. Dennis, D.D.) These figures do not include the Bibles sold by the ordinary publishers of Christian countries, nor the Bibles sold in Europe by Bible Societies. If it were possible to gather all the statistics, we may be certain the figures would amount up to five or six millions. What a book that must be, which circulates in 454 languages, and is sold at the rate of 5,000,000 copies per annum !

The relation between Jehovah and Israel was a peculiarly tender one ;—" When Israel was a child, then I loved him, and called my son out of Egypt,"[1] says Jehovah by the mouth of one of His prophets. As Israel was Jehovah's son, he had to be taught, trained, disciplined. The history of the people, then, is simply the record of Jehovah's dealings with them in this process of loving and patient training.

Israel's education was chiefly in the hard school of experience, in national disaster and disgrace, in national recovery and victory. But not in events alone : Jehovah spoke His will out clearly through a series of most remarkable men known as the PROPHETS. What is most noticeable in these men is the direct- ness and the certainty of the message they brought from Jehovah to His people. Usually it was criticism and condemnation, with a definite declaration of coming punishment , but now and then it was comfort and consolation, with the promise of speedy help and relief.

It would be most interesting to trace the history in detail and to watch how the people were led step by step to fuller and clearer knowledge of God, but we must not stay for that here. We need only say sufficient to enable readers to understand the cir- cumstances in which the great prophecy which we wish to discuss came to be uttered.

The people were slaves in Egypt. They were brought out under Moses ; and in the peninsula of Sinai a Covenant was made between them and Jehovah, which laid the foundation of their religion and their national life. Joshua was their leader in the conquest of Palestine, an event which probably took place in the thirteenth century B. C. During the first two centuries of their residence in the land they had no settled form of government, but acknowledged as their rulers from time to time certain great personalities known as Judges. Towards the end of the eleventh century the pressure of the Philistines led to the establishment of a monarchy. Saul knit the people together ; David built up a petty empire ; Solomon gave his attention to commerce and internal organization.

---

[1] Hosea, ii, i.

But after these three reigns the nation fell in two. From 937 B. C. onward for two centuries, instead of one state there are two rival kingdoms, the northern called Israel and the southern Judah. The great events of these centuries occur in Israel. Through the prophets Elijah and Elisha the people were taught that Jehovah would never consent to be one among many gods : *They must worship Jehovah alone.* Later, Amos prophesied that Jehovah would bring about the destruction of the kingdom of Israel, because the people would not live righteously. They offered God sacrifices, while He demanded righteous conduct between man and man. But they could not believe that Jehovah would destroy His own chosen people . " How can we believe that He will destroy the only people in all the world that He has made Himself known to ?" Swift comes the answer, "You only have I known of all the families of the earth · therefore I will punish you for all your iniquities."[1] Israel had had greater privileges than any other people ; therefore Israel had a deeper responsibility, and would receive a severer punishment. In 722 B. C. the Assyrians overthrew Israel, and carried away 27,290 of the leading inhabitants and settled them in Mesopotamia and Media.[2] The prophecy of Amos was thus literally fulfilled.

The kingdom of Judah, which was not involved in the fate of Israel, stood for rather more than a century longer. Isaiah was the prophet of Jehovah in Judah when Israel fell. He condemned his own people just as Amos had condemned Israel, because they identified religion with ritual, and would not give Jehovah what He wanted, namely, righteousness. The state of the people was so bad that Isaiah declared that nothing could cure them. Jehovah would intervene : the bulk of the people would be destroyed, but *a righteous remnant would be saved.* Towards the end of Isaiah's life Sennacherib, king of Assyria, came, devastated the land of Judah, took many of the cities, and demanded the surrender of the capital, Jerusalem. Isaiah advised

---

[1] *Amos*, 3,2 .

[2] 2 *Kings*, 17, 1-23 ; the figures are from an inscription of Sargon, the victorious Assyrian King : see *Authority and Archæology*, 101.

the king not to yield, and prophesied that the Assyrian would not be able to touch the city. His prophecy was fulfilled to the letter. The huge Assyrian army was suddenly annihilated by some unknown cause, probably pestilence, and Sennacherib hastened back to Assyria.[1]

A century later Judah was in a still worse condition : idolatry, polytheism, immorality were eating out the vitals of the nation. In 604 B. C. Jeremiah prophesied that Jehovah would bring Nebuchadnezzar, king of Babylon, into Syria, and that he would destroy Judah and all the nations round about, that they would groan under the rule of Babylon for seventy years, but that at the end of that period Jehovah would punish the Babylonians for their iniquity, and would make their land desolate forever.[2] But his countrymen would not listen. Jehovah had saved His people from the Assyrian in the time of Isaiah · why should He allow the Babylonian to touch them now ? Yet in 585 B. C. Nebuchadnezzar took Jerusalem, burned the city and the temple, and carried away the king and all the leading families to Babylon[3]. Once more the word of Jehovah, as spoken by His prophets, was literally fulfilled.

But what was to be the end ?—Jehovah seemed to have utterly destroyed His chosen people : what was His purpose ? what good was to come out of it ?

The people of the northern kingdom, carried away in 722 B C , soon lost their religion, and were in consequence speedily lost themselves among the peoples of the East. Not so the captives of Judah : the training of Isaiah and his disciples and of Jeremiah and his friends had taken fast hold of their hearts, so that even in a foreign land, far away from home and temple, they held by the religion of Jehovah. Nor is that all : they began to take their religion seriously ; they began to perceive that the prophets were right in declaring that Jehovah was a very different God from the gods of the nations around them, that He would not be satis- fied with sacrifice and song, but demanded *heart-worship and*

---

[1] *2 Kings*, 19, 35—36; Wellhausen, *Israel and Judah*, Chap. VII; *Authority and Archæology*, 105-108.

[2] *Jeremiah*, 25, 1-14.　　　　[3] *2 Kings*, 25, 1-22.

righteousness. But although they clung to their faith in Jehovah, they were naturally greatly depressed by the seeming hopelessness of their captivity.[1] To rebel against the Babylonians, and by the sword regain their freedom and their land, was an utter impossibility : they were altogether helpless under the omnipotent empire

But about 550 B C. Cyrus, an Elamite king, began a great career of conquest. In 549 he overthrew the Cimmerians under their king Astyages, and by 546 he was master of Persia. He then went further west to subdue Asia Minor.[2]

It was at this juncture, according to all scholars, that a great prophet, whose name is unknown. began to comfort and encourage the Jewish exiles in Babylon. His prophecy is preserved for us in the latter part of the book of Isaiah.[3] His message is that the sufferings of the exiles are nearly at an end, that Cyrus is to capture Babylon and give them leave to return to their native land.[4]

In 538 B. C. Cyrus marched into Babylonia, defeated the Babylonian army, and seized the city, thus fulfilling in a very striking way the second part of Jeremiah's prophecy.[5] Soon after, the Judean captives received permission to return to Palestine. They were also allowed to carry with them the sacred vessels which Nebuchadnezzar had carried away from the temple in Jerusalem.[6] The prophecy of restoration was thus triumphantly fulfilled One company of exiles went at once, and others followed them later.

The people of Jehovah in this way began life afresh after the great national punishment of the Captivity. They had thoroughly learned one lesson at least, namely, this, that *Jehovah spoke through His prophets.* So in their new system, while they retained the old ritual of the temple, they made careful provision for the preservation of the writings of the prophets and for the instruction of the people in the Mosaic Law.

---

[1] *Psalm* 137.

[2] The details have now been read in Cyrus's own inscriptions Hastings, *Dictionary of the Bible*, I, 541.

[3] From Chap. 40 onwards. *See* Driver, *Introduction*, 217.

[4] *Isaiah*, 40, 1-10; 44, 24-28.

[5] *Authority and Archæology*, 123-126.   [6] *Ezra*, Chap. 1.

We need trace the history no further; for it was this post-exilic Judaism, with its great care for the Scriptures, and its energetic attempts to instil them into the minds of the people, that formed the environment of Jesus and His work.

But we must now return to the great prophet who spoke consolation to the exiles in Babylon, and study his ideas. His conception of God is very lofty. He illustrates in many ways His holiness, His faithfulness, His tender sympathy, His omnipotence, His absolute sway among nations, and His power of foretelling future events by the mouth of His prophets. On the other hand, the prophet's conception of the duty and destiny of the people of Jehovah is correspondingly high. Israel has been created and chosen by Jehovah, and therefore is precious in His sight; but He did not choose them out of favouritism, nor was it His purpose to heap blessings on them merely for their pleasure and aggrandizement. Israel is *the Servant of Jehovah* The service they have to render is to reveal God's character and purposes to all the nations of the earth. This is the end of their election and of their long training. But, as in the past the nation has fallen far short of Jehovah's ideal, so now in Babylon the people as a whole is very far from fit for the work which God has for them to do: "Who is blind but my servant? or deaf as my messenger that I send?"[1]

Consequently there is a further choice within the chosen people. The use of the title, the Servant of Jehovah, is narrowed. The prophet knows that God's ends will be worked out, that through Israel Jehovah's name will be carried to the ends of the earth; he also sees as clearly that the nation as a nation is unfit for this lofty duty; so he recognises that the Servant who shall do this work will be found within the people. Whether he identified the Servant of Jehovah in this narrower sense with the small group of really God-fearing men who formed the soul of Israel in his own day, or whether he thought of an individual to be specially prepared for the task by Jehovah, we do not know. Most probably this point was not clear to the prophet himself.[2]

---

[1] *Isaiah*, 42, 19.
[2] For the ideas of this great prophet, see *the Cambridge Bible for Schools, Isaiah*, Vol. II, pp. XXII—XXXIX.

It is in four poems of peculiar dignity and surpassing spiritual penetration that this narrower use of the title occurs. In the first[1] of these Jehovah describes His Servant's character and work; in the second[2], the Servant tells how Jehovah prepared him for his task; in the third,[3] we have a portrait of the Servant as a martyr; while in the fourth[4], he is represented, though righteous himself, as dying a shameful death as an atonement for the sins of the unrighteous. It is to this fourth poem that we would direct the attention of our readers.

THE ATONING DEATH OF THE SERVANT OF JEHOVAH.

Jehovah.—

> Lo, My Servant shall deal wisely ;
> He shall rise, be uplifted, and be exalted exceedingly.

> Even as many were amazed at him,—
> So marred from a man's was his appearance,
> And his form from that of the sons of men !—
> So shall he startle many nations ;
> Before him kings shall shut their mouths.
> For what had not been told them they shall see,
> And what they had not heard they shall consider.

Israel.—

> Who believed what was heard by us ?
> And the arm of Jehovah, to whom was it revealed ?

> He grew up like a sapling before us,
> And like a shoot out of parched ground.
> He had no form, nor majesty, that we should look upon him,
> Nor appearance, that we should desire him.

> He was despised and forsaken by men,
> A man of pains and familiar with sickness ;
> And as one from whom men hide their face
> He was despised, and we held him of no account.

---

[1] *Isaiah*, 42,1-4.   [2] *Isaiah*, 49,1-6.   [3] *Isaiah*, 50,4-9.   [4] *Isaiah*, 52, 13—53, 12.

Yet it was our sicknesses that he bore,
And our pains that he carried ;
While we accounted him stricken,
Smitten by God, and afflicted.

But he was pierced because of our transgressions,
Crushed because of our iniquities ;
Chastisement to secure our peace was laid upon him,
And through his stripes healing came to us.

We all like sheep had gone astray,
We had turned each one to his own way ;
And Jehovah made to light on him
The iniquity of us all

The Prophet.—

He was oppressed, yet he let himself be afflicted,
And opened not his mouth,
As a lamb that is led to the slaughter,
And as a sheep that is dumb before her shearers,
And opened not his mouth.

By a tyrannical judgment he was taken away ;
And, as for the men of his time, who considered,
That he was cut off out of the land of the living,
That for the transgression of my people he was stricken ?

And his grave was made with the wicked,
And his tomb with the unrighteous,
Although he had done no violence,
And there was no deceit in his mouth.

But it was Jehovah that willed to crush him,
That laid on him sickness :
If he should lay down his life as a guilt-offering,
He would see a posterity, he would lengthen his days,
And the will of Jehovah would prosper by his hand ;
After the travail of his soul he would see it,
And would be satisfied with his knowledge.

Jehovah.—

> My Servant the righteous one, shall make many righteous ;
> For he shall bear their iniquities.
>
> Therefore I will give him a share with the many,
> And with the strong he shall divide the spoil ;
> Inasmuch as he poured out his life-blood to death,
> And let himself be numbered with the transgressors ;
> Yet it was the sin of the many he bore,
> And for the transgressors he interposed.

In this marvellous poem we have four successive vignettes of the Servant. There first rises in the prophet's mind a vision of the awe-struck wonder with which the nations and their kings shall gaze on the Servant of Jehovah, when after unequalled humiliation he shall be uplifted in surpassing glory The next picture takes us back to his life of humiliation · he grows up with nothing in him to strike the eye or attract the attention of men ; nay, rather all turn their back on him as worthless, contempt- ible, smitten with divine punishment   But along with this sorrowful portrait there comes the passionate confession of the men of Israel, that the Servant in all his sufferings had been bearing their sins. The third picture shows us the suffering Servant in uncomplaining meekness enduring a criminal's death with all its shameful associations ; yet this death is explained as occurring in accordance with God's will, and as being a guilt- offering. The series ends in triumph the righteous Servant by bearing iniquity will make many righteous and will achieve the glory and the reward of the conqueror

In this prophecy the remarkable thing is that the sufferings and death of the Servant are construed throughout, not as a martyrdom, but as much more. In his death he lays down his life as a guilt- offering ; and all his sufferings, inclusive of his death, are, from Jehovah's point of view, chastisement laid on him on account of the sins of others, from the Servant's point of view, a voluntary bearing of their iniquities. His willingness to endure and his meekness under oppression are very vividly put before us ; but God's purpose to crush him is insisted on with equal em- phasis. The awful tragedy happens within Israel · but after it is

consummated, the Servant, once so despised, neglected and oppressed, startles the nations, and kings in amazement shut their
mouths in his presence. The purpose of the dread sacrifice is
TO BRING MEN TO RIGHTEOUSNESS ; and that end, we are told,
will be widely accomplished.

Whence did the prophet draw the ideas of his prophecy ? If
any piece of literature bears signs of inspiration, this does , but the
experience which enabled him to become the vehicle of inspiration in this particular case may also be conjectured. The sufferings, which many of the prophets, and especially Jeremiah, had
endured at the hands of their fellow-countrymen, had made a
profound impression upon the best minds in Israel ; and the
affliction of the exiles in Babylon was manifestly not merely
penal, but also purificatory.

CHAPTER IV.

VIRGIL'S NEW AGE OF JUSTICE AND PEACE.

THE slow but steady rise of an obscure inland Italian town, first
to the rule of all Italy, and finally to imperial sway over the whole
Mediterranean world, is as full of problems for the intellect as of
fascination for the imagination   Whence the extraordinary vigour
and practical genius of this city?   What gave it so much capacity
in comparison with any other Italian town?   Does the secret lie
in the Roman character, the Roman intellect, or in the constitution
of the republican city itself?   But other questions still more serious press for answers   How did the Roman government affect the
subject provinces ?   How did it react upon the Roman character
and upon the life of the capital?   Could a single city furnish men
of character and ability in sufficient numbers for such a prodigious
task?

The answer to these grave questions must be sought in the
history of the last century of the existence of the republic.   From
about 145 B C to about 48 B C Rome was never at rest . violent
political strife, faction, proscriptions and civil wars eclipse everything else in the internal history of the imperial city during these
years.   The old state machinery was getting worn out ; the old
families, corrupted by the immeasurable success of the Rome
which was their making, were grinding the provinces by their
cruelty and greed, and would not budge an inch from their privileges, nor indeed lift a finger, to save Rome and Italy from the
moral and economic ruin with which they were threatened   The
wrongs of the slave, the Italian and the provincial cried aloud for
redress ; scarcely less urgent was the need for the introduction
of a great deal of fresh blood into the governing classes ; but
the latter were utterly hostile to every change   Hence the violent

struggles throughout the century between the Government and the other classes. The empire had proved too much for the old Roman character.[1] The only force that remained really efficient was the army.

Who shall describe the ruin, bloodshed, misery, desolation, wrought by these years ? The national character suffered a frightful fall also · corruption in public, immorality in private, became all but universal The weariness and the hopelessness generated by the seemingly unending strife made men forget their old passion for freedom and sigh even for tyranny, if only it would bring peace.

Relief came when Julius Cæsar crushed Pompey at Pharsalus in B. C. 48. There was fighting here and there for two years more, but it was of little consequence. Pharsalus made Cæsar the monarch of Rome He lived barely four years after his victory; for the daggers of the conspirators found his heart on the 15th of March, 44 B. C , yet by a series of masterly administrative and legislative acts he laid in great broad lines the foundation of the new empire and set in motion the healthy forces that were needed for the regeneration of Rome and Italy. His work is Titanic both in conception and execution. Seldom has such a great man executed such a mighty task

But his murder loosed all the old fiends again, and they worked wilder woe than ever. For now the whole gigantic empire was drawn into the whirlpool, and the provinces were only a little less miserable than Italy During Cæsar's own struggle his mighty genius and his magnanimity had thrown a glory upon the murky clouds of the storm ; but now that the sun was set, black darkness settled over the unhappy empire [2]

There was a pause in the strife, when, in B C. 40, a treaty was drawn up between Octavian and Antony at Brundisium and confirmed by the marriage of Antony to the sister of Octavian. Men hoped that the end had come at last and that the world would enjoy a lasting peace.

---

[1] Froude, *Cæsar*, 12-19.

[2] For the whole picture *see* Mommsen, especially the very last page of his history.

It was during this bright moment that Virgil, who later was to write the *Aeneid*, and so earn for himself a very great name in European literature, composed a short poem, which finds a place among his Pastorals, and is named *Pollio* Here is a translation of lines four to twenty-five, which will be found quite sufficient to bring the main ideas of the poem before us —

"The last epoch of the Sybil's prophecy has come at length, the great series of the ages is being born anew, at length the virgin, Justice, is returning, returning too the reign of Saturn; at length a new race of men is being sent down from heaven high. Do thou, Lucina, but smile thy chaste smile upon a boy with whose coming at last ceases the iron race and the golden springs up throughout the world, do so, Lucina. it is thine own Apollo that now reigns. It is in thy consulship, Pollio, that this glorious age will come in, and the months of the great year will begin their march. Under thy leadership all traces that remain of Roman crime in civil strife shall pass away, and passing, free the lands from constant fear.

" He shall receive the life of the gods, and shall behold gods and heroes mingling together, and himself shall be beheld by them; and with his father's virtues he shall rule the world at peace.

" Unasked the earth shall shower upon thee, sweet boy, thy first baby gifts, the gadding ivy with the fox-glove, and lily-bean entwined with smiling bear's-foot. The goats shall bring home uncalled their milk-filled udders, the harts shall no longer fear great lions, and flowers shall spring to caress thee where'er thou liest down. The asp shall perish; the treacherous, poison herb shall perish too, and everywhere shall spring Assyrian balm."[1]

The Greeks and Romans had a great system of cycles and ages, not unlike the Hindu Kalpas and Manvantaras. One cycle follows another, the beginning of each being marked by the sun, moon and stars all occupying their original positions. The Roman phrase for cycle is "great year." Each great year is subdivided into "months," that is ages The first age of each great year is the golden, when Saturn reigns, and a divine race of men occupies the earth; the last is the iron age, when Apollo reigns, and men are sinful.

Virgil declares, then, that the end of the old cycle has come, and that the new cycle is about to begin with all the splendour of the golden age. Saturn will reign; Justice and Peace will return to the earth; a god-like race of men will spring up all over the world ; nature will be redeemed ; and primitive simplicity and innocence will reappear. Idyllic scenes of peace and plenty— trade and manufacture all forgotten—give the poem a wonderful charm

The most outstanding idea of the prophecy, however, is that the new age opens with the birth of a boy, who is to receive special divine help, and is to be at once the pattern and the prince of the new time   Who the boy was that Virgil had in mind, the critics have not been able to decide.[1] Clearly he was a son born in 40 B. C. to one of the leading Romans ; but we can say no more. Evidently Virgil believed that the civil wars were over, that a new era of peace had begun, and that this boy might be looked forward to as the ruler who should effectively transform the empire, revive primitive virtue and simplicity, and banish the foul demon war forever

His prediction was not verified · no boy born in 40 B. C. became a world-ruler and regenerator ; and, besides, nine long years of doubt and fear, horror and blood, had to be endured, before Octavian became, by the battle of Actium, the acknowledged master of the Roman world ; and, while he completed the task of Cæsar, and succeeded in doing the work of a great ruler in a marvellous fashion, no one would dream of saying that he fulfilled the ideal of this poem

It is an unfulfilled prophecy ; yet it is not without interest and value for men to-day. First of all it is of interest as a revelation of the ideas and the hopes that filled men's minds in Virgil's time. " The anticipation of a new era was widely spread and vividly felt over the world ; and this anticipation—the state of men's minds at and subsequent to the time when this poem was written—probably contributed to the acceptance of the great political and spiritual changes which awaited the world."[2] But it is of still greater interest as a revelation of what Virgil himself thought, Virgil, who was perhaps the purest and most interesting personality in the Græco-Roman world then. Men generally were looking for a regeneration of the world , we have here

[1] Sellar, *Virgil*, 146 , Simcox, *Latin Literature*, Vol. I, 257.
[2] Sella· ʼ· ·, , ʼ᛭ ᛭, *l·* ᛭ᛧ ᛭ ᛧᛍᛦᛧ᛭ ᛧ

Virgil's own thoughts on the great subject. He shared with
others the idea that the world was on the verge of the dawning of
a new day, a day of renewed justice and peace ; but he had an
idea of his own, that of a great personality, a man of high moral
character, specially endowed by the gods for his great task as
leader and ruler of the new time. Scarcely less prominent is his
idea of the nobler race of men that shall spring up in the new
era. It is no picture merely of good government such as
Augustus gave the world that we have here ; but a prophecy of
the moral regeneration of mankind under the influence of a
divinely prepared leader.

CHAPTER V.

JESUS OF NAZARETH

I   The difference between ancient and modern times in Europe is vital.   Human society is never stagnant ; development in one direction or another is constant ; so that in the course of a few centuries changes, both numerous and noticeable, take place everywhere   Thus the Europe of the middle ages differs very markedly from the Europe of to-day   Yet the one is the direct outcome of the other   On the other hand, the civilizations of Greece and Rome, although we owe them an incalculable debt, are marked off from modern civilization by differences which can only be spoken of as essential   For it is not any single element that‧ has been added externally to ancient life so as to produce modern society ; it is rather a subtle spirit, which has modified all thinking,⟩ altered the values of things, produced organic changes in⟩ government and society, and recreated art and literature   The unexampled development of   science and invention, and the extraordinary activity and vigour of European commerce and arms, which are often spoken of as the chief characteristics of modern civilization, are rather to be regarded as indications of unparalleled vitality and efficiency in the social organism than as essential products of its spirit   Science and invention flourished among the Greeks ; the Roman empire was as vigorous as any modern state in matters of war.   These things prove the healthy vitality of the society of the West ; its essential spirit is to be sought elsewhere.

A comparison of ancient and modern life reveals differences at once very numerous and greatly significant.   The economics of Europe have been revolutionized ; for the labour, the manufacture and the commer   f an ert   m e‧ rested on a i. i‧ of

slavery [1] Government has been turned upside down ; for the ruling
principle of ancient politics was hereditary and exclusive citizen-
ship in a city-state ;[2] while modern politics have been created by
the great principles of the equality of men irrespective of birth
or station and the indefeasible sovereignty of the people [3] In
ancient society human life as such had no value . infanticide was
practised openly by all as a right and proper thing necessary for
the well-being of the family and the state ;[4] prisoners taken in
war, if not killed, were made slaves, and as slaves their lives and
persons were absolutely at the mercy of their masters ;[5] aliens
had a place in the state only on sufferance : society stood in no
relation to them and had no duties towards them [6] The social
organism of modern times, on the other hand, is a new creation,
produced by the conception of the inherent sanctity of human
life and the divine dignity of the human personality [7] Modern
education is in form and method Greek ; but the results it
produces are altogether new ; first, because it carries the modern
spirit within the ancient forms, and secondly, because modern men
regard education as part of the birthright of every human being
Moral ideals show very important differences, chiefly in the
direction of the elevation of humility, meekness, sympathy,
forgiveness and self-sacrifice, and the extraordinary advance in the
conception of the right of individual freedom. In ancient times
the individual citizen had no rights as against the State ;[8] now we
demand not only freedom in matters of profession and business,
as against caste restrictions, but intellectual, moral and religious liberty. The differences between ancient and modern
religion are very extraordinary in many ways. For the present
we need only note the one far-reaching distinction, that to the

---

[1] See article *Slavery* in *Encyclopædia Brittanica* , and *cf.* Gibbon, Chaps.
II and XXXVIII, Cunningham, *An Essay on Western Civilization in its
Economic Aspects* , Wallon, *Histoire de l'Esclavage dans l'Antiquité.*

[2] Fowler, *The City-State of the Greeks and Romans* , Mahaffy, *Social
Life in Greece*, 44 ; Kidd, *P.W.C.*, Chap. VI.

[3] Kidd, *P. W C.*, Chaps. VII to IX.   [4] Kidd, *P. W. C.*, 190, 223-4.

[5] Sohm, *The Institutes of Roman Law* , Wallon, *Histoire de l'Esclavage
dans l'Antiquité*   [6] Bury, *History of Greece*, I, 72.

[7] Kidd *P. W. C.*,   [8]

ancients religion was a *political duty*, which the citizen was bound to fulfil, and a *civic privilege*, which only those in whose veins ran the sacred blood of the community could share ;[1] while modern religion is the loftiest activity of the human spirit, as far transcending the narrow limits of the State as it does the petty distinctions of race and blood   The differences, then, between ancient and modern life are not accidental but essential

A second thing to be noticed is the altogether unexampled vitality and pervasiveness of modern civilization. During the nineteenth century alone, while the population of the rest of the world remained nearly stationary, the actual numbers of the European peoples rose from 170,000,000 to 500,000,000 [2] Here is physical life on a gigantic scale   Let readers think, next, of the extraordinary advances made during the nineteenth century in every province of natural science, from mathematics and physics up through the biological sciences to psychology and the science of religion, the swift upward progress made in literary, historical and philosophical method, and the innumerable inventions that have been produced for facilitating every form of human activity. Are not these facts evidence of an amazing store of intellectual vitality in the society of the West? Think also of the buoyancy, the hope, the youthful delight in action, the glance into the future, which characterize the progressive peoples of Europe and America. Colonization, on the other hand, exploration, missions, world-wide commerce, domination over other races, whether you call them bad or good, are incontestable proofs of energy, physical, moral and intellectual. Further, these forms of vital orce are clearly of the greatest practical importance in the world   In the process of natural selection which, whether we like it or not, is ceaselessly being carried on among the races of mankind, the possession of such energy is one of the crucial factors in the struggle   But this civilization has also an altogether unique power of entering into other civilizations and working revolutionary changes there . its pervasiveness is almost as

---

[1] Kidd, *P. W. C.*, 160-172 , Seebohm *The Structure of Greek Tribal Society*, 4, 138.
[2] Sir Robert Giffen *Address to the Manchester Statistical Society*, 15.

remarkable as its vitality. We need only point to India and
Japan to-day for proof of this.

Western civilization, then, is a thing by itself, not more
clearly distinguished from ancient life than from the civilizations
that have arisen in other parts of the world. What is it that has
made the difference? What subtle spirit is it that appears in
every aspect of the civilization, that assumes so many forms, and
generates such transcending energies?

There can be but one answer: it is Christianity In every
community religion is the life principle, the central fire, which
fills the whole with living force, and communicates its own spirit
to every cell of the organism.[1] That is a law which is becoming
ever more apparent in all anthropological, sociological and
religious science From this general law we might conclude in
this particular case. that it is the religion that gives the civilization its character But we need not appeal to general principles ;
history tells us in the clearest tones that the peculiarities which
distinguish Western civilization from every other spring directly
or indirectly from the Christian faith.

Now one way of classifying religions is to divide them into
two groups, spontaneous and founded The former are results of
the united unconscious action of a tribe or people : for example,
the religions of Greece and Rome The latter spring from some
particular man, and are inseparably connected with his life . for
example, Buddhism, Christianity and Mohammedanism

That Christianity is a founded religion, and that it springs
from Christ, admits of no question Tacitus, the Roman historian,
in speaking of the great fire at Rome in 64 A. D., which devastated
ten of the fourteen districts into which the Imperial city was divided, says that the people got their heads filled with the suspicion,
that the Emperor himself (Nero was then on the throne) had used
his agents to set the city on fire He then continues :—

"Consequently, to get rid of the report, Nero fastened the guilt and
inflicted the most exquisite tortures on a class hated for their abominations,
called Christians by the populace Christus, from whom the name had its
origin, suffered the extreme penalty during the reign of Tiberius at the
hands of one of our procurators, Pontius Pilatus, and a most mischievous

---

[1] Kidd *Social Evolution* Chaps. IV & V.

superstition, thus checked for the moment, again broke out not only in Judea, the first source of the evil, but even in Rome, where all things hideous and shameful from every part of the world find their centre and become popular Accordingly, an arrest was first made of all who pleaded guilty ; then, upon their information, an immense multitude was convicted, not so much of the crime of firing the city, as of hatred against mankind Mockery of every sort was added to their deaths Covered with the skins of beasts, they were torn by dogs and perished , or were nailed to crosses, or were doomed to the flames and burnt, to serve as a nightly illumination, when daylight had expired.

Nero offered his gardens for the spectacle, and was exhibiting a show in the circus, while he mingled with the people in the dress of a charioteer or stood aloft on a car. Hence, even for criminals who deserved extreme and exemplary punishment, there arose a feeling of compassion ; for it was not, as it seemed, for the public good, but to glut one man's cruelty, that they were being destroyed."[1]

Christ, then, is a historical person He was a Jew ; He founded Christianity ; and He was executed by Pontius Pilatus during his procuratorship of Judæa, i e, between 27 and 37 A D[2] Other facts enable scholars to fix the date of His death within narrower limits . a few adopt 30 A D, but by far the greatest number prefer 29 A. D. ;[3] and that date we adopt here.

Here, then, are the facts . Christ was put to death by the Roman Governor of Judæa in 29 A. D , but this did not extinguish Christianity ; for it spread not only in Judæa but beyond ; so much so, that in 64 A. D "an immense multitude" of Christians were found in Rome, and were for their faith put to death with horrible barbarities.

Such is the first chapter of the history of Christianity in Europe. From this point onwards the facts are well known The furious hostility visible here in the spirit of the Roman Empire against the Christian faith ended in the victory of the latter, in its gradual acceptance by the races of Europe, and the continuously increasing infiltration of Christian ideas into the minds of the people The process is far from complete ; for the contrast between the old spirit and the new is so extreme that

---

[1] Tacitus, *Annals*, XV, 44, Church and Brodribb's translation.

[2] Church and Brodribb's *Annals*, 374.

[3] For all the facts and the opinions of various scholars, *see* Hastings, *Dictionar of th B·b'e*, I 110-415

only long ages of discipline and the slow processes of evolution
will suffice to work the transformation. We have seen how
essentially different the spirit in our modern life is from the spirit
of Græco-Roman life. how much greater would be the contrast,
if one were to oppose the pure spirit of Christ to the spirit of
Paganism! When men accept Christ, they are conscious of the
authority of His perfect character and His heavenly life, and they
know that He claims their complete submission to Him; but
they have no idea how far-reaching this claim is Christ demands
that not only every part of the individual's life—thoughts, feelings,
words. deeds—but every aspect of social and political life as well
should be made subject to His law of love. This is easily stated.
how hard is it to work it out, except in a long series of generations!

But imperfect as has been the perception of Christ's aims,
and still more imperfect the execution of these by the peoples of
Europe, yet the results of even their very partial submission to them
have been, as we have seen, momentous in the highest degree.
Christ has made modern Europe

Now we found from our study of Virgil's prophecy that he
believed that a new age was just about to open Like other
thinking men of his day, he felt that the civilization under which he
lived was played out, that new life was needed, new morals and a
fresh organization of society He believed that in the new age the
leader and king would be a great Roman, and that under him the
world would be transformed

Further, it is sufficiently striking that, while his prophecy
received no literal fulfilment, yet the new age did actually begin
shortly after the time when he wrote, an age which has produced
a new race of men, new moral ideas and an altogether fresh
organization of society, and vitality and virility, besides, such as
Virgil never dreamed of He spoke of a great leader favoured of
the gods, a noble Roman The new age did come in under the
guidance of a new leader, but he was no aristocratic Roman, but
a Jew, and a man of the people, Jesus of Nazareth

II Christ's name and life are well-known outside Christen-
dom. He is spoken of in very high terms in the book which all
Mohammedans revere · and contact with the West has brought a

certain amount of knowledge about him to the peoples of India, China and Japan. Now the most striking fact in this connection is this, that while most of these Mohammedans, Hindus, Buddhists, and Confucians condemn Christians violently, and many write against Christianity, *they one and all speak with the highest praise of the character of Christ* The same is true of sceptics and agnostics in Christian lands. One might compile a most fascinating volume consisting merely of extracts from non-Christian writers, in which Christ is spoken of as the best of men, as the ideal man, as the man whom all men should not only admire, but imitate.

Now we have in this a most remarkable fact. There is no other character in history that is so universally revered. There is no other man whom all men join in praising with so much heartiness. Charles Lamb speaks for the human race when he says . "If Shakespeare were to enter this room, we should all spring to our feet ; if Christ were to enter, we should all fall on our knees."

But HE WAS CRUCIFIED This, the purest and noblest of men, was subjected to the most shameful form of death possible. Nor was there only the bare execution every circumstance that could make death bitter to the noble human spirit was added He was betrayed by one of His own chosen Twelve ; the remaining eleven deserted Him ; one plucked up heart and followed at a distance, but only to deny him Indeed the universal breakdown of human character around Him is one of the saddest things in history. The Jewish priests and scribes, the common people, the Roman Governor and the common soldiers, all reveal their worst passions in the presence of Christ, while He stands amongst them in all the silent majesty of innocence [1]

We here quote three short paragraphs from St. Matthew's Gospel [2] The first describes what took place after the members of the Jewish Sanhedrin had decided that Jesus deserved to be put to death .—

"Then did they spit in His face, and buffet Him ; and some smote Him with the palms of their hands, saying, Prophesy unto us, Thou Christ who is he that struck Thee ?" [3]

---

[1] *Matthew*, Chapters 26 & 27.

[2] For the criticism of the Gospels *see* below, pages 49-50.

[3] *Matt*. 26 to 68

Then those model judges carried their prisoner before Pontius
Pilate, the Roman Governor, and after much persuasion got him
to condemn Jesus to death, when the following scenes took
place:—

"Then the soldiers of the Governor took Jesus into the palace, and
gathered unto Him the whole band. And they stripped Him, and put on Him
a scarlet robe. And they plaited a crown of thorns and put it upon His head.
and a reed in His right hand ; and they kneeled down before Him, and
mocked Him, saying, ' Hail, King of the Jews ! ' And they spat upon Him,
and took the reed and smote Him on the head   And when they had mocked
Him, they took off from Him the robe, and put on Him His garments and
led Him away to crucify Him "[1]

" And as they came out, they found a man of Cyrene, Simon by name :
him they compelled to go with them, that he might bear His cross. And
when they were come unto a place called Golgotha, that is to say, The place
of a skull, they gave Him wine to drink mingled with gall . and when He had
tasted it, He would not drink   And when they had crucified Him, they parted
His garments among them, casting lots   and they sat and watched Him
there. And they set up over His head His accusation written, THIS IS
JESUS THE KING OF THE JEWS   Then are there crucified with Him
two robbers, one on the right hand, and one on the left   And they that
passed by railed on Him, wagging their heads, and saying. ' Thou that
destroyest the temple and buildest it in three days, save Thyself · if Thou art
the Son of God, come down from the cross.' In like manner also the chief
priests mocking Him with the scribes and elders said, ' He saved others .
Himself He cannot save. He is the King of Israel , let Him now come down
from the cross, and we will believe on Him. He trusteth on God ; let Him
deliver Him now, if He desireth Him : for He said, I am the Son of God.'
And the robbers also that were crucified with Him cast upon Him the same
reproach '[2]

How was it that of all men Jesus should be the man subjected to all this ? How can we reconcile His character and His
destiny ?

Let us recollect what Plato had written 400 years earlier —

" The just man will be scourged, racked, fettered, will have his eyes
burned out, and at last, after suffering every kind of torture, will be
crucified "

Now we do not insist on the correspondence in detail between
the words of Plato and the death of Christ, although that, while

---

[1] *Matt.*, 27, 27-31.   [2] *Matt* , 27, 32-44,

not complete, is sufficiently remarkable ; but we wish to em-
phasize, with all possible force, this most extraordinary fact,
that Plato foresaw that a man of the character of Jesus would
suffer as He did.

How are we to explain the fact? What is the reason why
the men of Christ's day treated this most humane of men with
such barbarous inhumanity? The answer is that it was inevitable.
Jesus is the revelation of the uttermost holiness of God, and *His
attempt to lay that standard upon the human spirit*[1] roused to its
utmost fury against Him all the sinfulness of our common human
nature. It is the same contest of which we are each conscious
in our daily life between inclination and conscience ; only, in the
case of Jesus, it seems as if all the little battles of every individual life had met in one gigantic struggle between sinful human
nature and its Lord. And the same struggle necessarily continues
wherever Christianity goes   The persecutions of the Roman
Empire are merely the external signs of the convulsive efforts of
the spirit of Paganism to resist the march of the Spirit of God
In every land Christ is met by the same opposition   Everywhere
selfishness, self-interest and passion dissuade men from following
the Man of Sorrows ; and the struggle is there, terrible in its
reality and intensity, even if it never break out into open persecu-
tion. But, in surveying these surging battles, the careful observer is
much struck with this fact, that, while human passions inevitably
fight against Christ, yet He has in Conscience an ally, which neither
by bribes nor by bullying can be made to desert Him. He is
the objective conscience of the human race. He is Plato's just
man.

III   Let us now try to realize what kind of a being the
founder of Christianity was. Our chief sources of information
are the Gospels ; for from the other books of the New Testament
and from outside literature we learn only scattered facts about
His life on earth. We shall not appeal to the fourth Gospel, for

[1] It was not the *teaching* of Jesus, but His *interference*, in the interests of
His own supreme standards, with the traditional worship and customs of the
Jews, that led the Jewish hierarchy to determine on His death. See below
p. 52.

4

there are still numerous questions with regard to it unsettled, but shall confine ourselves to Matthew, Mark and Luke, books recognized on all hands as of high historical value, and as having been written between 65 and 95 A.D [1] Anyone may very speedily convince himself of the splendid historical reliability of these simple narratives. From Josephus and other Jewish writers of the first and second centuries, and from casual remarks in Greek and Roman books, we are able to learn what the life of these days was like ; [2] but nowhere do we get such vivid, detailed, realistic pictures as in the Gospels. "They are full of feeling for the time ; they understand its men, schools, classes, parties ; they know the thoughts that are in the air, the rumours that run along the street ; they are familiar with the catchwords and phrases of the period, its conventions, questions, modes of discussion and style of argument. And all is presented with the utmost realism, so grouped round the central figure as to form a perfect historical picture, He and His setting being so built together as to constitute a single organic whole " [3]

How then does Christ appear in them ? — His name was Jesus ; [4] Christ is a title springing from his teaching, as we shall see. He lived in the small town of Nazareth, in the district of Galilee [5] in Palestine, and worked as a carpenter there. [6] At length, in 26 A.D., He gave up carpentry and began His public career as a preacher. [7] The picture given of Him in the Gospels is a most attractive one. Wherever He goes, the sick, the suffering, the distressed crowd around Him. Blind beggars, outcast lepers, hopeless paralytics, even uncontrollable lunatics, receive help from His healing power He feeds the hungry, breathes hope into the downcast, lifts up the enfeebled patient, helps the helpless. But while every form of suffering and sorrow appeals to His compassion, His heart is set on winning the souls of men. So we find Him preaching in the synagogue and by the sea, on the

---

[1] See Hastings, *Dictionary of the Bible, ad loca*, and Moffatt, *Historical New Testament*, pp 272-274. The most probable dates are, for *Mark*, 66 to 70 A.D., and for *Matthew* and *Luke*, 70 to 75 A.D

[2] See the masses of evidence gathered in Schurer, *H J. P.*

[3] Fairbairn, *The Philosophy of the Christian Religion*, pp. 328-9.

[4] *Mark*, 1, 9. [5] *Mark*, 1, 9. [6] *Mark*, 6 . [7] *Luke*, 3, 1 ; 4, 14.

mountain-side and in the busy street, now stirring vast crowds now dealing with an individual, and again pouring His rich teaching into the ears of the chosen Twelve No man ever had such power of convincing men of sin and leading them to repentance: the simple fisherman,[1] the fallen woman,[2] the wealthy custom-house officer[3] and the dying robber,[4] all felt condemned in His presence, and through Him entered into the new life.

The character revealed in His words and deeds is beautiful beyond comparison. The most outstanding feature of it is His love for God and the perfect and unbroken serenity of His intercourse with Him Love for man also shines out everywhere. But the most extraordinary point is this, that He in whom the moral ideal was so lofty, so deep and so broad, He who was so keenly conscious of sin in others, and had such power to make them feel it, betrays absolutely no consciousness of sin Himself, never asks for pardon, and never speaks of having repented, or of having passed through any crisis of the nature of conversion.[5] On the other hand the perfect balance of His character is almost as marvellous as His sinlessness · judicial severity controlled by perfect love ; supreme authority that is also supreme gentleness ; strength filled with tenderness ; regal dignity shown in acts of lowliest service ; holiness that led Him among the unholy ;(sublimest self-consciousness, never leading to anything but self-effacement and self-sacrifice. ' And yet again, is there anything about Him so wonderful as His power of winning human love? The Gospels are full of instances of it, and to-day how many millions of men, women and children would count it a supreme joy to die for His sake !

His teaching is a perfectly articulated and unified whole, as may be seen from the scientific studies of it that have been published during the last twenty years.[6] But we must not attempt to deal with that fascinating subject here, except in so far as the whole is implied in what He says about Himself. For it is only

---

[1] *Luke*, 5, 8. [2] *Luke*, 7, 36-50. [3] *Luke*, 19, 1-10. [4] *Luke*, 23, 39-43.

[5] See Harnack, *What is Christianity*, pp. 32—35.

[6] See specially Weiss, *N. T. Theology*, Beyschlag, *N. T. Theology ;* Wendt, *Teaching of Jesus*, Stevens, *Theology of the New Testament*, Robertson, *Our Lord's Teaching ;* and many others.

that part of it, namely, His account of Himself and His mission, that we propose to touch on.

We shall understand it best, if we begin with what happened at His crucifixion ; for it was only at the end of His life that He made perfectly clear to the whole world what His claims were People often wondered whether He were not THE CHRIST, *i e*, *The Messiah*, the Anointed One, the great national deliverer whom the Jews were so earnestly expecting and praying for ;[1] but during the three years of His public life He seldom openly made the claim [2] When, however, He went to Jerusalem for the last time, He made a royal entry into the sacred city,[3] cleansed the Temple from the desecration of its cattle-market,[4] and began to teach in the Temple courts,[5] thus by both word and act publicly claiming recognition as the Christ.

The Jewish leaders had been often bitterly incensed by His teaching and His actions before His bold seizure of authority now decided them · they resolved on His death.[6] He was apprehended[7] and brought before the Sanhedrin,[8] *i.e.*, the High Court of Judæa Evidence was led against Him, but it proved very unsubstantial ;[9] so the High Priest, the president of the court, formally asked Him, " Art thou the Christ, the Son of God ? " and He answered in the affirmative.[10] Since they did not believe His claim, they could only come to the conclusion that He was an irreligious impostor, impiously arrogating divine authority to Himself Consequently they declared that He ought to be put to death for blasphemy against God [11]

But the Sanhedrin could not put anyone to death ; the sanction of the Roman Governor was necessary.[12] He was therefore dragged before Pilate Here they did not charge Him with

---

[1] See Schurer, *H. J. P.*, Div. II, Vol. II, pp. 126 ff.

[2] The reason for His silence is to be found in the fact that the Messianic hope, as popularly held, had become largely political: to have confessed Himself a the Christ would have been to precipitate a revolt against Rome   Cf. McGiffert's *Apostolic Age*, 28

[3] *Matt* , 21, 1-11.   [4] *Matt.*, 21, 12-17.   [5] *Matt.*, 21. 23—23, 39

[6] *Matt.*, 26, 3-5.   [7] *Matt.*, 26, 47-56.   [8] *Matt* , 26, 57 and 59.

[9] *Matt.*, 26, 59-62.   [10] *Matt.*, 26, 63-64.   [11] *Matt.*, 26, 65-66.

[12] Sch r H. J. P., , II, Vo'. I, 13⁸ ; J   , 1⁸   .

blasphemy, but with rebellion against the Roman Emperor. 'The King of the Jews' was a synonym for 'the Christ'; so they argued that Jesus, in claiming to be the Christ, claimed the sovereignty of the Jews, and was therefore guilty of rebellion against Tiberius.[1] Pilate knew perfectly well that the Jewish leaders were jealous of Jesus, and that the charge was a mere pretence;[2] his Roman sense of justice revolted against the execution of an innocent man; and he wished to save Him; but they played upon his fears, and finally succeeded in wringing a condemnation from him.[3] It was because the Roman soldiers were struck with the extreme absurdity of the idea of Jesus being a rival of Tiberius, that they got up their pitiable comedy of a court, and did Him mock homage as King of the Jews.

So He was led away to Calvary and crucified, and above His head on the cross was written, in three languages (Hebrew, Greek and Latin), the charge against Him,—

JESUS OF NAZARETH, THE KING OF THE JEWS.

Thus Jesus took good care that there should be no doubt as to what He claimed to be : He did not write a book, nor cut an inscription on a rock, *but He let Himself be crucified*, that all men to the end of time might know that He claimed to be the Christ [4]

*   *   *   *   *

Now let us see what He meant when He called Himself the Christ. To get to understand this fully would be to learn the complete meaning of His teaching; for it is such a perfect organism that every member of it is closely related to every other member; yet we may gain sufficient insight for our purpose from a broad survey.

The subject of the whole teaching of Jesus was *the Kingdom of God*. He held that God had been working from the very beginning for the winning of man to Himself, and that especially among His own people Israel He had shown His hand They had not only come to know Him as the God of righteousness whose law was holiness; they had enjoyed His love; they had experienced His mercy and His power to redeem. But

---

[1] *Matt.*, 27, 1-2; 27, 11.   [2] *Matt.*, 27, 18.
[3] *M "., 27, 11 26*   [4] McGiffert's *Apostolic A., 27-22.*

with the coming of Jesus Himself a new era of the world had
opened : [1] God was now drawing near to all men, in a new relationship of love and mercy, with the purpose of saving them.[2]
This was the coming of the Kingdom of God.[3] The history of
Israel had been a long discipline in preparation for this [4] On the
ground cleared in Israel, and on the basis of the revelation already
made to them, God would now reveal Himself to all men. The
destiny of Israel—" I will give thee for a light to the Gentiles " [5]—
would now be fulfilled.[6]

God, then, was about to enter into a new relationship with the
whole human race. That new relationship would be, like the
old one with Israel, characterized not only by His righteousness,
but by His redeeming love His eternal purpose, which had been
in contemplation all through the centuries of Israel's training, would
now be unfolded. The childhood of the world was over : its first
simple lessons had been learned ; the real business of Time could
now be begun The partial unveiling of God's face which it had
been Israel's privilege to behold would now become a full revelation in the sight of the nations The King of Israel would be seen
to be the Father of men. Further, as Israel had learned her
lessons through Jehovah's redemptive acts at the Red Sea, on
Zion, and in Babylon, so mankind would learn the Father's love
through the great redemptive acts involved in the coming of the
Kingdom

The chief conviction that Jesus had about Himself was that
in and through and by Him the Kingdom of God was coming:
this it was that constituted Him THE CHRIST. His self-consciousness is the most marvellous phenomenon within the compass
of history ; there is nothing else comparable with it The
primary element in it seems to have been the knowledge that He
was the true man, man as God wishes Him to be, faultless both
morally and religiously.[7] Closely connected with this is another
element, quite as unparalleled in human experience, a feeling of

---

[1] *Mark*, 1, 15.
[2] See the parables in *Matt.*, 22, 2-14 , and *Luke*, 14, 15-24.
[3] *Mark*, 1, 15.   [4] *Matt.*, 11, 13-14 , *Luke*, 16, 16.
[5] *Isaiah*, 42, 6 ; 40, 6.   [6] *Matt.*, 24, 14 , 26, 13 ; 28, 19.
[7] *Matt.*, 11, 25 &.

close kinship to all men, a consciousness of solidarity with the
whole race and of personal connection and sympathy with every
individual.[1] These two elements of His nature—His perfection as
man, and His relationship to the race as a whole—He summed up in
the phrase which He used so often to describe Himself, THE SON
OF MAN.[2] Correspondent to this double relationship to man
stands a double relationship to God first, He stands in the closest
personal kinship to God—the Son with the Father— ; so that He
alone can reveal God, and God alone can reveal Him ;[3] and
secondly, He is God's representative to the human race[4] This
dual relation to God He expressed by calling Himself THE SON
OF GOD[5]

The life of a being of this order, standing in great, pregnant
relations to God on the one hand and to the human family on
the other, would necessarily be of transcendent significance. So
we find that He regarded His own words and acts and all the
great experiences of His life as of supreme importance in the
history of the world[6] His coming opens a new era ;[7] His public
life is a wedding feast in the otherwise grey experience of men ;[8]
His teaching is the final revelation of God ;[9] His acts are glimpses
of the divine activity ;[10] His death, which to the casual observer is,
but a coarse judicial murder, is the solemn sacrifice that ratifies the
establishment of the new relationship between God and man.[11]

Since such were the chief convictions Jesus held about
Himself and His mission, *authority* was naturally the chief note
of His teaching. His hearers marked that characteristic at the
very outset ;[12] and a modern student cannot fail to be impressed
with it as he reads the Gospels He states quite frankly that
He has come to fulfil the law and the prophets ;[13] He sets up His

[1] *Matt.*, 25, 40 ; 25, 45.
[2] See *e.g.*, *Matt.*, 9, 6 , 11, 19 , 12, 8 , 16, 13 , 20, 18 , 20, 28 , 25, 31 ; 26, 64.
[3] *Matt* , 11, 27 ; 16, 17 ; 17, 5.
[4] *Matt.*, 21, 37 , 11, 10 , *Mark*, 8, 37-38 ; 9, 37 ; *Luke*, 10, 16.
[5] *Matt.*, 3, 17 , 17, 5 , 26, 63-64 , 21, 37 , 22, 41-45 , *Luke*, 10, 22.
[6] *Luke*, 10, 23-24.   [7] *Mark*, 1, 15   [8] *Matt.*, 9, 15 , 22, 2-14.
[9] *Luke*, 10, 22.   [10] *Luke*, 11, 20.   [11] *Matt* , 20, 28 , *Luke*, 22, 20.
[12] . . . .

own "I say unto you" not only against the Jewish traditions,[1] but against the definite provisions of the Mosaic law ;[2] and over and over again He demands from men such love, faith, submission, obedience, as can be rightly given only to a Divine Master.[3]

In Jesus of Nazareth, then, we have a historical person, whose time and environment are well known to us, and whose teaching and life also stand out clear and unmistakable ; and the most prominent thing about Him is this, that, by word and deed, and finally by His crucifixion, He made it clear to all men that He claimed to be both Son of Man and Son of God.

Here, then, we have the secret of that similarity which we are all so clearly conscious of, when we read a Gospel alongside of the *Gītā*. In the Gospels we have in historical form the authoritative utterances of the historical Jesus ; in the *Gītā* we have the imaginations of a poet-philosopher who was clear-sighted enough to realize that an incarnate god would have many things to say about himself, and that his teaching would bear the note of authority. When, however, we look for exact parallels between the two, they are hard to find . the books are so utterly diverse in origin and teaching that they have little in common except the tone of the master. In a few cases, however, the resemblance is rather striking : here, then, we place side by side the words of Jesus and the imaginations of the writer of the *Gītā*.

SAYINGS OF JESUS.	VERSES FROM THE GITA
All authority hath been given unto me in heaven and on earth *Matt.*. 28, 18.	Nature gives birth to movables and immovables through me, the supervisor, and by reason of that the universe revolves. IX, 10.
All things have been delivered unto me of my Father : and no one knoweth who the Son is, save the Father ; and who the Father is, save the Son, and he to whomsoever the Son willeth to reveal him *Luke*, 10, 22	I know the things which have been, those which are, and those which are to be ; but me nobody knows. VII, 26.

[1] *Matt.*, 5, 44 , 15, 20.   [2] *Matt* , 5, 32 , 5, 34 ; 5, 39 , 15, 11 , 19, 7-9.
[3] .· . . . . . 10, ·7·, 4 1 , ·.² , ·. , .

SAYINGS OF JESUS.	VERSES FROM THE GITA.

Come unto me, all ye that labour and are heavy laden, and I will give you rest. *Matt.*, 11, 28.

Forsaking all duties, come to me as thy sole refuge. I will release thee from all sins : do not grieve. XVIII, 66

But that ye may know that the Son of Man hath authority on earth to forgive sins,—*Mark*, 2, 10

Of all mortals, he who knows me to be unborn, without beginning, the great lord of the world, being free from delusion, is released from all sins. X, 3.

If any man would come after me, let him deny himself, and take up his cross, and follow me   *Mark*, 8, 34.

In thought renouncing all actions unto me, intent on me, applying thyself to the yoking of thine intellect, be thou always thinking of me. XVIII, 57.

So, therefore, whosoever he be of you that renounceth not all that he hath, he cannot be my disciple. *Luke*, 14. 33

Having thyself yoked by the yoke of renunciation, thou shalt come to me. IX, 28.

Come unto me, all ye that labour and are heavy laden, and I will give you rest. *Matt.*, 11, 28

In him seek shelter with all thy might . by his grace thou shalt attain supreme peace, the eternal dwelling-place. XVIII, 62.

If they have called the master of the house Beelzebub, how much more shall they call them of his household? *Matt.*, 10, 25.

——hating me in their own bodies and in those of others. XVI, 18.

And blessed is he, whosoever shall find none occasion of stumbling in me. *Matt*, 11, 6

Deluded people,..... not knowing my highest nature as great lord of entities, disregard me, as I have assumed a human body. IX, 11.

My yoke is easy, and my burden is light. *Matt*, 11, 30.

To the constantly-yoked Yogi, who constantly remembereth me, never thinking of another, I am easy of access. VIII, 14.

Learn of me   *Matt.*, 11, 29

Learn of me   XVIII, 59

It would lead us far afield to set forth in detail all the striking things that Jesus has to say about His own person and mission, but it may be well to quote a few passages exhibiting lines of character and thought not exemplified above :—

(*a*) His meekness and lowliness.

"I am meek and lowly in heart." *Matt.*, 11, 29.

(*b*) The conditions of His earthly life.

"The foxes have holes, and the birds of heaven have nests , but the Son of Man hath not where to lay His head " *Luke*, 9, 58.

(*c*) The necessity that He should die for men

"And He began to teach them, that the Son of Man must suffer many things, and be rejected by the elders, and the chief priests, and the scribes, and be killed, and after three days rise again." *Mark*, 8, 31.

(*d*) His spirit of service and self-sacrifice

"Even as the Son of Man came not to be ministered unto, but to minister, and to give His life a ransom for many *Matt*, 20, 28.

"But I am among you as he that doth serve." *Luke*, 22, 27

(*e*) His claims on the allegiance and love of men

"Every one who shall confess Me before men, him shall the Son of Man also confess before the angels of God : but he that denieth Me in the presence of men shall be denied in the presence of the angels of God." *Luke*, 12, 8-9.

"He that loveth father or mother more than Me is not worthy of Me ; and he that loveth son or daughter more than Me is not worthy of Me." *Matt.*, 10, 37-38.

(*f*) His universal sympathy.

Inasmuch as ye did it unto one of these My brethren, even these least, ye did it unto Me." *Matt.*, 25, 40.

(*g*) His declaration that he will return to judge all men.

"Many will say to Me in that day, Lord, Lord, did we not prophesy by Thy name, and by Thy name cast out devils, and by Thy name do many mighty works ? And then will I profess unto them I never knew

you : depart from Me, ye that work iniquity." *Matt.*,
7, 22-23.

(*h*) His presence with his followers

"For where two or three are gathered together in My
name, there am 1 in the midst of them." *Matt.*,
18, 20.

* * * * *

The *Gītā* is one of the most eloquent possible proofs of the
fact that the human heart cries out for an incarnate Saviour.
Scarcely less impressive is the evidence furnished by the reception
of the *Gītā* by Hindu readers . not the greatest of the Upanishads, neither the *Chāndogya* nor the *Katha*, has had one
quarter of the influence exercised by this late poem , and the secret
undoubtedly is to be found in the attraction of the man-god
Krishna. How many generations of pious readers have found in
the story of the life and teaching of the incarnate god something
to which their deepest and most persistent religious instincts have
responded ! How many to-day turn to Krishna in their trials and
troubles !

On the one hand, then, we have the imaginative portrait of
Krishna, surrounded by millions of adoring worshippers—touch-
ing spectacle ! On the other, stands the historical Jesus of Nazareth, Son of Man and Son of God, stretching out His nail-pierced
hands to India, as He says, "Come unto Me, all ye that labour
and are heavy laden, and I will give you rest." Rightly read, the
Gītā is a clear-tongued prophecy of Christ, and the hearts that
bow down to the idea of Krishna are really seeking the incarnate
Son of God.

IV. We have been able to see some little distance into the
self-consciousness of Jesus, and to realize in part at least that
on which He grounds His claim to the heart of every man ; but
we have not yet learned the secret of that most marvellous of
His powers, His power to win human love. To that we must
now address ourselves.

It is a well-known fact of history that, shortly after the death
of Christ, His followers began to preach in His name, and that
very soon the new faith began to spread rapidly. We have already
learned from Tacitus that in ʻ4 A. D. there was "an immense

multitude" of Christians in Rome itself. Now the greatest of all the early missionaries was Paul. He was the apostle of Europe. We mention his name here, because we wish to refer to one of his Epistles. These letters are the earliest of our Christian documents The series begins with two brief letters, both written, with a short interval between them, to the church at Thessalonica. The most probable date for them is 49 A. D , that is, only twenty years after the death of Christ But the letter we wish to use is one sent from Ephesus to the church of Corinth[1] about 55 A D.,[2] that is, twenty-six years after the death of Jesus We must not stay here to speak of the splendour of the ethical feeling and teaching of the Epistle further than to say that it manifestly has its source in Jesus We must direct our attention to other facts which appear in it.

Christianity, we note, has already spread from Judæa into the provinces of Asia[3] and Galatia[4] in Asia Minor, and Macedonia[5] and Achaia[6] in Europe. Phœnicia, Syria, Cilicia and Cyprus are not mentioned ; but we know from other sources[7] that they too were already evangelized Thus in twenty-six years the Church of Christ has become a great organization, extending through many lands, yet conscious of its unity in Christ[8] We note also that then, as to-day, BAPTISM is a solemn ceremonial act, in which a man through the action of the Holy Spirit becomes a member of the body of Christ,[9] while THE LORD'S SUPPER is a recurrent feast, in which the members of the Church have fellowship with the Lord and with each other[10]

But what we would call special attention to is *the place assigned to Christ* in tne Epistle With reference to the Christian, Christ is THE LORD,[11] with reference to the Father, He is THE SON ;[12] He is spoken of as the Lord of Glory,[13] the Power

---

[1] *I.e., I Corinthians.*

[2] For the dates of Paul's Epistles, see the articles in Hastings's *Dictionary of the Bible*, or Moffatt's *Historical New Testament*, 121—137.

[3] 16, 19.   [4] 16, 1.   [5] 16, 5.   [6] 16, 15.

[7] *Acts*, 11, 19 , *Galatians*, 1, 21-24.   [8] 12, 13,   [9] 12, 13.

[10] 11, 20-34 ; 10, 16-17.

[11] Very frequent cf. 1, 2 ; 1, 3 ; 1, 7 , 8, 6 , 12, 3 , 16, 22. *The Lord* takes in the Epistles the place held by *the Son of Man* in the Gospels.

[12] 1 .   [13] ...

of God,[1] and the Wisdom of God ;[2] and prayer is offered to Him.[3] All spiritual authority and power are attributed to Him.[4] The Church is His body,[5] and He supplies His grace and power to every member [6] He will come back again to earth in glory,[7] and will then reveal all secrets and judge all men.[8]

But there is another point still more noteworthy, and that is *the way in which the crucifixion of Christ is interpreted.* Instead of regarding that judicial murder as a regrettable incident, like the assassination of Cæsar or the death of Socrates, Paul and his fellow-believers glory in it,[9] not only as the crowning event of the divine revelation made in Christ, but as the consummation of His work as the Saviour of men [10] Paul makes it the basis of all his preaching,[11] and in it he finds all the wealth of spiritual wisdom which Christianity contains.[12] He contrasts the wisdom of God wrapped up in that divine tragedy with the worldly wisdom of earthly rulers.[13]

What can be the explanation of this extraordinary attitude to such an event ?—The basis of it is the solemn declaration, which Paul makes in the Epistle, and which he says he made to his converts first of all, that ON THE CROSS CHRIST DIED FOR OUR SINS.[14] The crucifixion, as a bare event in history, is but an act of wicked folly on the part of the rulers of Judæa ; but, viewed from the standpoint of morality and religion, it is a divine act of world-wide significance In the blood of Christ a new covenant had been made between God and man [15] This is the Gospel, which all the Apostles teach, and which all the churches believe.[16] Through faith in Christ, on the basis of this tremendous assertion, the Corinthian Christians, like the rest, had been saved,[17] *i.e.,* they had received *the forgiveness of their sins*[18] and *the sanctifying Spirit.*[19] They thus no longer belonged to themselves : they had been bought with a great price, the blood of

[1] 1, 24.   [2] 1, 24 ; 1, 30.   [3] 1, 2.   [4] 5, 4 ; 7, 10 ; 14, 37 ; 15, 24-28.
[5] 12, 12-13 ; 12, 27.   [6] 1, 4-7 ; 1, 30 ; 3, 5 , 12, 5 ; 16, 23.
[7] 1, 7 ; 4, 5 ;   [8] 4, 5.   [9] 1, 17-18.   [10] 11, 23-26 ; 15, 3.
[11] 1, 18 ; 1, 21 ; 2, 2 ; 15, 1 ; 15, 11.   [12] 1, 22-24.   [13] 2, 6-8.
[14] 15, 3.   [15] 11, 25.   [16] 15, 1 ; 15, 2 ; 15, 11.   [17] 1, 18 , 1, 21.
[18] 15, 17.   [19] 1, 2, 1, 30 ; 3, 16 , 6, 11 , 6, 19.

the Son of God.[1]   They were no longer part and parcel of heathen society ; each one was a member of the body of Christ.[2]

What led Paul and all the other Apostles and all the early Christians to form such an extraordinary theory ?   How did they come to the conclusion that the crucifixion was not a squalid tragedy, but a divine sacrifice ?   This letter tells us quite plainly ; the reasons were these · Jesus Himself declared before He was crucified, that *His death was to be the basis of the New Covenant,*[3] and this declaration of His *had been divinely confirmed by His Resurrection*[4]

Now mark : this letter was written within twenty-six years of the event.   The majority of the twelve Apostles, and multitudes of other men who had known Jesus, were still alive.[5]   Paul's good faith is beyond all question ; and, as he was intimate with Peter and John and the rest of the Apostles, and also with James the brother of Jesus,[6] he had access to the very best information possible   Further he had been one of the most violent opponents of Christianity.   His testimony is, therefore, evidence of the, very highest value   We may conclude, then, with the utmost certitude that we are standing on an immoveable historical foundation, when we say that *Jesus, before His crucifixion, said He was about to die for the sins of men.*

But this evidence does not stand alone.   It is a historical fact, acknowledged by scholars of every school, that all Christian churches have from the very beginning celebrated the Lord's Supper.[7]   Now this universal usage in so many churches, divided not only by long distances but in many cases also by minor differences in doctrine, cannot be explained at all except as a result of a command of Jesus Himself.   If any single disciple had started such a practice, it could never have won its way to universal acceptance.   Now consider the significance of this fact : Jesus, on the night in which He was betrayed, took bread, broke it, and bade His disciples eat it, saying, ' This is My body.'   He

---

[1] 6, 19 ; 7, 23.   [2] 6, 15 ; 10, 17 ; 12, 12-13 ; 12, 27.
[3] 11, 23-25. Cf. *Jeremiah*, 31, 31-34.   [4] 15, 4 compared with 15, 14.
[5] 15, 6.   [6] *Galatians*, 1, 18—2, 10.
[7] See McGiffert's *Apostolic Age*, 536

then took a cup of wine and bade them drink it, saying, ' This is
My blood.'¹ The scene is absolutely without a parallel in the
history of the world ; and it can have but one meaning, *viz* , that
Jesus regarded His death as a sacrifice

But the direct statement of Paul is corroborated, not only by
the institution of the Supper, but also by this fact, that the doctrine, that Christ died for our sins, is an integral part of the
teaching of Jesus as that is handed down to us in the Gospels.
We have already seen that He held that His death was necessary
for the establishment of the Kingdom. We must now set out His
teaching on this subject with a little more fulness. We shall
restrict ourselves to a single Gospel. In the earliest saying that
refers to it, His death is a future event, coming inevitably, and
destined to bring sorrow to His disciples. " And Jesus said unto
them, Can the sons of the bride-chamber mourn, as long as the
bridegroom is with them? but the days will come, when the
bridegroom shall be taken away from them, and then will they
fast."² In the next it is much more clearly defined. Its necessity
is emphasized ; we are told that the agents are to be the religious leaders of Israel ; and it is to be followed by the resurrection. " From that time began Jesus to shew unto His disciples,
how that He must go unto Jerusalem, and suffer many things of
the elders and chief priests and scribes, and be killed, and the
third day be raised up."³ Twice over this same prophecy is
repeated, the last time with more detail.⁴ Then follows a
most striking saying, in which He speaks of His death as voluntary : it is a giving away of His life ; and it is explained as the
climax of His life of service ; for the gift is 'a ransom for many,'
that is a price paid, in order to redeem many from sin. " The
Son of Man came not to be ministered unto, but to minister, and
to give His life a ransom for many."⁵ We need not linger over
the next sayings, though each has its own interest.⁶ The last
saying occurs in the account of the institution of the Supper. In
these words He teaches in the clearest way, first, that His death

---

¹ The event is described in *Matt.*, 26, 26-30 ; *Mark*, 14, 22-26, and *Luke*,
22, 14-20 , as well as in 1 *Corinthians*, 11, 23-26.
² *Matt.*, 9, 15.   ³ *Matt.*, 16, 21.   ⁴ *Matt.*, 17, 22-23 ; 20, 17-19.
⁵ *Matt.*, 20, 28.   ⁶ *Matt.*, 21, 39 ; 26, 2 ; 26, 12.

is to be the ground of forgiveness, and secondly, that after His death He is to be the source of the spiritual life and strength of His followers. "And as they were eating, Jesus took bread, and blessed, and brake it ; and He gave to the disciples, and said, 'Take, eat ; this is My body.' And He took a cup, and gave thanks, and gave to them, saying, 'Drink ye all of it ; for this is My blood of the covenant, which is shed for many unto remission of sins."[1] The teaching of Jesus is an organic whole, and is incomplete without this, His own interpretation of His death of shame.

Jesus, then, gave Himself up to death as the sacrifice for the sins of men. Our Christian documents go on to declare that *He rose from the dead on the third day*, and that this resurrection of His was God's confirmation of the sacrifice of His Son. That men should at first sight disbelieve the astounding assertion, that the crucified Jesus rose from the dead, is not to be wondered at ; but *the fact remains*. Sceptical scholars have laboured for centuries to explain away this extraordinary occurrence, but no one of these scholars themselves will venture to say that any explanation hitherto given is satisfactory. The latest attempt, that made by Schmiedel in the *Encyclopædia Biblica*, is a farcical failure. The following are the adamantine facts which no rationalism has ever yet succeeded in crushing or melting :—(*a*) the Christians declared that they had seen Christ and spoken with Him after His resurrection ; (*b*) they were absolutely sincere in this belief[2] ; (*c*) the Christian Church arose as a result of this conviction ; (*d*) the grave was empty. The account of Christ's appearances given in the fifteenth chapter of our Epistle is well worth study. Those who wish to look into this question further may consult Ballard's *Miracles of Unbelief*, pp. 135 ff

We have thus, by a serious historical inquiry, reached the conclusion, that Jesus of Nazareth, the founder of the Christian religion, declared, before His crucifixion, that He was about to die for the sins of men, and that this assertion of His was sealed with the divine approval by the unique miracle of the resurrection. We have also seen that this was *the Good News*, which Paul and all the other Apostles preached, and on which the early Church was

[1] *Matt.* 26, 26 ff.   [2] Now universally acknowledged

founded. It is this that has won for Jesus the love of myriads ; it is this that has been the magnet to draw them away from sin. It is the source of the joy and vital power of the Christian life.

Now let us recollect the poem upon *The Servant of Jehovah*, which we considered in our third chapter. How marvellously Jesus corresponds to the extraordinary idea which that poem discloses, the despised and oppressed prisoner who endures in un-complaining meekness the uttermost shame of a violent death, and is finally recognized as having been "pierced because of our trangressions, and crushed because of our iniquities." That any-one should write such a poem, seems strange in the extreme ; that Jesus should have fulfilled it, is infinitely more wonderful.

How comes it that this Jewish carpenter, with His three years of public life and His cross of shame, fulfils so many ideals and aspirations ? He brings in the new age which Virgil and his contemporaries sighed for ; He is Plato's just man ; He utters from His own self-consciousness such things as the author of the *Gītā* imagined an incarnate god would say ; He gives Himself up to death, in sheer love, as a sacrifice for sin, thus fulfilling the deepest needs of man, as expressed by the old Hebrew seer ; and He is the only human being whom men of every race and clime can heartily admire and unhesitatingly imitate. Nor is this all: many other convergent lines of thought might be suggested, in the light of which Jesus stands out as the ideal of our common humanity and the fountain of the love of God.

How is all this to be explained? Wide chasms sever the Hindu sage, the Greek philosopher, the Hebrew prophet and the Roman poet ; yet in Jesus their several ideals are reconciled in a loftier unity. Once in the course of the centuries East and West have actually met l Nor was the meeting merely the resolution of antitheses in a wider conception : what the Jew and the Indian, the Greek and the Roman, dreamed of as the unattainable, that Jesus actually accomplished in this work-a-day world of ours, amid storms of the cruellest hatred and calumny.—What is your candid opinion about Him, brother ? How are you to solve the problem raised by His life, death and place in history ? Can He be better described than in His own words, SON OF MAN and SON OF GOD ?

APPENDIX.

NEO-KRISHNA LITERATURE.

The Neo-Krishna movement is about twenty years old. Before 1880 Vaishnavism does not seem to have been in great favour with the higher castes of Bengal. Traditionally they were Saivas or Sāktas rather than Vaishnavas ; and English education, which bore very heavily for half a century on every form of Hinduism seems to have told with peculiar severity on Krishnaism. But shortly after 1880 a great change becomes visible . Krishna begins to be praised on every hand, and ancient Vaishnava books are read and studied with avidity. The new movement seems to have owed its origin, on the one hand, to the teaching and influence of Ramkrishna Paramhansa, Keshub Chundra Sen, Bijoy Krishna Goswami and Shishir Kumar Ghose ; and on the other, to the efforts of two or three noteworthy literary men, who threw themselves into the task of painting the character of Krishna with extraordinary enthusiasm. The *Gitā* at once leaped into greater prominence than ever : numberless editions and translations of it have been published. Many essays have appeared comparing Krishna with Christ and Vaishnavism with Christianity. Thus a large Krishna literature, both in English and Bengali, has sprung up. The following seem to be the more important books of this literature :—

1884   Essays in *Prachār* on *Krishnacharitra* by Bunkim Ch. Chatterji.

1886   1. *Krishnacharitra*, Bunkim Ch. Chatterji, 1st edition. A volume in Bengali prose on the character of Krishna.

1887   2. *Raivatak*, Nobin Ch. Sen. An epic poem in Bengali on Krishna's youth.

1887   3. *The Bhagavad Gītā, or the Lord's Lay*, Mohini M. Chatterji. An English prose translation of the text and of parts of Sankara's commentary. An attempt is made to put the *Gītā* on the same level as the New Testament.

1888   4. *Krishna Jivani*, Prosanna Kumar Vidyaratna. A life of Krishna in Bengali prose.

1889   5. *Srikrishner Jivana O Dharma*, Gaur Gavinda Ray. The life and religion of Krishna from the standpoint of the New Dispensation : Bengali prose.

1890   6. *Srimadbhagavadgītā*, Krishnananda Swami (i e Krishna Prasanna Sen). The text in the Bengali character with a Bengali commentary and translation.

1892   *Krishnacharitra*, Bunkim Ch. Chatterji, 2nd edition. This edition contains a great deal of new matter.

       7. *Amiya Nimai Charit*, Shishir Kumar Ghose. First part. A life of Chaitanya in Bengali prose.

1893   *Amiya Nimai Charit*. Second part.

       8. *Kurukshetra*, Nobin Ch. Sen. An epic poem in Bengali on Krishna at Kurukshetra.

1894   9. *The Landmarks of Ethics according to the Gītā*. Bulloram Mullick.

           Amiya Nimai Charit. Third part.

1895   10. *Kālā Chānd Gītā*, Shishir Kumar Ghose. A sort of Krishnaite Song of Solomon in Bengali verse. It is said to have been composed in 1888.

1896   11. *Srikrishna, his Life and Teachings*, Dhirendra Nath Pal. 3 vols.

       12. *Srikrishner Kalanka Kena?* Nava Kumar Devasarma. A Bengali prose defence of the character of Krishna.

       13. *The Bhagavad Gītā*, Annie Besant. New and revised edition. An English prose translation with an introduction and a few notes.

       14. *Prabhās*, Nobin Ch. Sen. An epic poem in Bengali on the later years of Krishna's life.

1897 15. *Lord Gaurānga*, Shishir Kumar Ghose, 1st volume
A life of Chaitanya in English prose, with a discussion of the doctrine of Incarnations.

1898 16. *Krishna and Krishnaism*, Bulloram Mullick.
Lord Gaurānga, 2nd volume.

17. *Hindu Theism*, Sitanath Tattvabhushan

18 *An Elementary Treatise on Universal Religion*
Kshetra Mohan Mukerji. The religion of the *Gītā*
is here put forward as the universal religion.

1899 19 *Incarnation*, Nanda Krishna Bose. This treatise
follows in most points the theory of Incarnation put
forward in *Lord Gaurānga*.

1900 20. *The Young Men's Gītā*, Jogindranath Mukharji. An
English prose translation with introduction and
notes.

21. *Srimadbhagavadgītā*, Prasanna Kumar Sastri, 2nd
edition. The text in the Bengali character, with
several commentaries, and a Bengali translation by
Sasadhar Tarkachuramani.

1901 22. *The Imitation of Sreekrishna*, S. C. Mukhopadhaya
A daily text-book, containing extracts in English
from the *Gītā*, the *Mahābhārata*, and the *Bhāgavat
Purāna*.

23 *Sree Krishna*, Muralidhur Roy. An account, in
English prose, of the life and character of Krishna.

24 *Srimadbhagavadgītā*, Bhudhur Chattopadhaya, 4th
edition. The text in the Bengali character, with a
Bengali commentary.

1903 25. A most elaborate edition of the *Gītā*, edited by
Damudar Mukerji, is being published in parts.

26 A Bengali verse translation of the *Gītā* by Satyendra
Nath Tagore is appearing in *Bhārati*.

This revival of interest in Krishna and his worship is clearly
part of the great national movement which has been so potent in

Bengal, religiously, socially and politically, these last twenty
years. This period has witnessed the appearance of the whole
Neo-Hindu movement, with its literature, lectures, societies and
missionary propaganda, the rise of the Indian National Congress
and of the social reform movement, the advance of native
journalism to its present extraordinary influence, and the establishment of the 'native unaided colleges, which have so seriously
changed the balance of influence in Higher Education.' Neo-
Krishnaism, then, is one result of the operation of that potent
spirit whereby India has become conscious of her unity, and her
sons have been roused to a vigorous defence of all that they have
inherited from the past. This rise of the national spirit, though
it may be troublesome in small matters to the rulers of India,
is undoubtedly the last and greatest justification of English rule ;
and, while, with its exaggerations and insincerities and follies, it
cannot fail to provoke criticism,[1] yet its power to awake self-
reliance, self-respect and the passion for freedom ought to win
for it the approval and the encouragement of all good men.

There can be no doubt that among the influences which
have produced Neo-Hinduism, Christianity is one of the most
potent, if not the chief   This is peculiarly evident in the case
of the Neo-Krishna literature we are discussing. In 1899 the
Bengal Librarian wrote, "There is no denying the fact that all
this revolution in the religious belief of the educated Hindu has
been brought about as much by the dissemination of Christian
thought by Missionaries as by the study of Hindu scriptures ; for
Christian influence is plainly detectable in many of the Hindu
publications of the year." But beyond this general influence,
which cannot fail to be noticed by anyone who will take the
trouble to read the volumes, it is, we believe, perfectly plain that
the very ideas which have given birth to the literature are the
result of Christian influence. A distinct taste for such books
as the Gospels has sprung up ; and men have come to feel the
need of a perfect character, such as Christ's is, for daily contem-

---

[1] Many of the wisest Indians have spoken out on this subject. The
latest utterance is an article on *Pseudo-Nationalism* in *the Indian Messenger*
for August 9th.

plation and imitation. The Neo-Krishna movement endeavours, to supply these needs from within Hinduism, offering the *Gītā* instead of the Gospels, and Krishna instead of Christ.[1]

Nobin Ch. Sen seems to have been the first to conceive the idea of a modern rendering of the character of Krishna ; for he laid the project before some of his friends in 1882[2] His famous epic trilogy, *Raivatak*, *Kurukshetra* and *Prabhās*, are the result of this pregnant thought But, while he and Shishir Kumar Ghose have done a great deal to popularize the movement, there can be no doubt that Bunkim Ch. Chatterji's *Krishnacharitra* has been by far the most influential volume in the whole of this literature. Gaur Gavinda Ray's work, *Srikrishner Jivana O Dharma*, is a piece of excellent characterization, and has won the high regard of many thoughtful men.

The books on our list fall into two classes, *Historical* and *Traditional.* In the Historical class there are only two volumes, Tattvabhusan's *Hindu Theism*, and the *Young Men's Gītā*. These two frankly acknowledge that the *Gītā* is a late book. In the *Young Men's Gītā*[3] its date is said to be a century or two before, or a century or two after, the Christian era ; while in *Hindu Theism*[4] the *Gītā* is regarded as the point of transition from the old Vedānta to the religion of the Purānas. The standpoint of these two books is thus thoroughly historical, but it necessarily implies the abandonment of the divinity of Krishna.

All the rest of the books on the list fall into the second class ; for they hold the traditional position about Krishna. Most of them make no attempt at criticism of the sources, but treat the *Mahābhārata*, the *Gītā*, the *Harivansa* and the Purānas as all historical and all equally trustworthy. A few of the authors,

---

[1] Many other signs of Christian influence might be noted : thus *the Young Men's Gītā* is a counterblast to a Christian edition of the Song, and it is besides most evidently arranged and printed in imitation of some tasteful edition of *the Imitation of Christ;* while *the Imitation of Sreekrishna* proclaims its origin by its very name.

[2] See an essay by Hirendra Nath Dutta, which originally appeared in *Sāhitya,* now republished as an appendix to Nobin Chundra Sen's *Kuru-kshetra.*

[3] p. 11.   [4] pp. 74—76.

however, state plainly their own critical conclusions, and two or
three enter into some discussion of the main problems   These
attempts at criticism are the most pitiable parts of the whole
literature. The talented author of *Srikrishner Jivana O Dharma*,
by far too sincere and candid to ignore the Puranic elements in
the sources, frankly confesses their presence ; yet, believing
these books to be genuine representatives of the age of Kurukshetra, he is driven to the extraordinary conclusion that the Vedic,
the Vedantic, and the Puranic ages were contemporaneous.[1]   The
late Bulloram Mullick, in discussing the eighteen Puranas, goes so
far as to say, " Whatever may be the views of European savants,
there is indubitable proof that some of these Puranas existed in
the eleventh or twelfth century before Christ."[2]   Even Bunkim
Chundra Chatterji himself not only unhesitatingly adopts Goldstucker's rash guess, that Panini's grammar was written before the
Brāhmanas and the Upanishads, but on the basis of that unwise
conjecture, pushes back Panini's date to the tenth or eleventh
century B. C.,[3] *i e*, four or five centuries earlier than the pre-
Buddhistic date which Goldstucker[4] wished to establish. Dhirendra
Nath Pal, seeing that Bunkim Babu found it so easy to leap over
a few centuries, goes a little further and suggests the twelfth or
thirteenth [5] But, indeed, without some such strange perversion
of history, it is impossible to construct an argument for the
authenticity of the *Gītā* and the historicity of the *Mahābhārata*
that shall have even the semblance of reason

We note next that of all the books of the second class,
Bunkim Chundra's *Krishnacharitra* is the only work that gives
any independent criticism · all the rest, with the single exception
of *Srikrishner Jivana O Dharma*, merely echo his arguments.
Thus Bunkim Babu's theory is the only one we need discuss.

Now the whole critical structure of the *Krishnacharitra*
rests upon the passage on pages 41 and 42, where the date of
Panini is discussed. Panini is pushed back to 1000 B. C. ; and,
the ' original ' *Mahābhārata* being earlier than Panini, we are

---

[1] p. 1.   [2] *Krishna and Krishnaism*, 16.   [3] *Krishnacharitra*, 42
[4] *Pānini, his Place in Sanskrit Literature*, 227.
[5] *rikrishna, his Life and Teaching   ·   ·   ·*

asked to believe that it was produced within a century or two of Kurukshetra, and that it is in consequence trustworthy historically. The whole argument thus rests on the date of Pānini.

We translate this important passage :—

"Goldstucker has proved that, when Pānini's Sūtra was composed, Buddha had not arisen. In that case Pānini must belong to the sixth century B. C. But not only that, in his time the Brāhmanas, the Aranyakas, the Upanishads and the other parts of the Vedas had not been composed. Apart from the Rig, the Yajur, and the Sāma Vedas, nothing else existed. Asvalāyana, Sānkhāyana and the rest had not appeared. Max Muller says that the age in which the Brāhmanas were composed began about 1000 B. C. Dr. Martin Haug says that that was the end of the age, and that it began in the fourteenth century B. C. Therefore, if we say that Pānini must belong to the tenth or eleventh century B. C., we do not say too much."

Now the first remark we make on this extraordinary piece of criticism is this, that Goldstucker and Max Muller are most unfairly conjoined to support a date which both of them would have indignantly repudiated. For Muller's date for Pānini is the fourth century B.C.,[1] and Goldstucker never proposed to push him further back than the sixth century ; indeed all that he claims is that he has brought forward evidence which affords a strong *probability* that Pānini preceded the origin of the Buddhistic creed.[2] Our next remark is that, though more than forty years have passed since Goldstucker's book appeared,[3] he has convinced no one that the Brāhmanas and the Upanishads are posterior to Pānini's grammar : opinions still differ as to Pānini's precise date, but no scholar to-day puts him before the Brāhmanas.[4]

Can the grounds for this unanimity among modern scholars be vividly set forth ? We believe they can. Here, as in our first chapter, we shall not attempt to fix a definite chronology, but shall simply aim at reaching *the relative age* of the great books we are

---

[1] *Physical Religion*, 76. [2] *Pānini, his Place in Sanskrit Literature*, 227.
[3] It was published in 1861.
[4] Macdonell, 430-431 ; Kaegi, 7 ; Max Muller, *Physical Religion*, 63-64 ; Haraprasad Sastri, *A School History of India*, 4-7 ; R. C Dutt, *Brief History of Ancient and Modern India*, 17, 27 ; Bohtlingk's *Pānini* (Leipsic, 1887) ; Weber, *Indische Studien*, V, 1-172 ; Hopkins, *R. I.*, 350 ; Buhler in *S. B. E.*, vol. II, pp. xxxv, xxxix-xlii ; Eggeling in *S. B. E.*, vol. xii, p. xxxvii ; Bhandarkar, *Early History of the Deccan*, 5.

dealing with ; and we shall not deal with the meaning of disputed passages, but shall rest the case altogether on the clear and prominent features of history which every one can appreciate. There is, then, first of all the great broad fact that the Sūtras depend on the Brāhmanas, and are, in general, posterior to them, and that *the language and style of Pānini's Sūtras show that he belongs to about the middle of the Sūtra period.*[1] All the detailed study of the last forty years *has gone to strengthen this stable conclusion.*

But there is another and still more conclusive proof that Pānini comes long after the early Brāhmanas *These ancient books are written in Vedic Sanskrit.*[2] The early Upanishads are more modern in character, but even they belong to a stage of the language a good deal earlier than the Sūtras : Professor Macdonell's words are, "the oldest Upanishads occupying a position linguistically midway between the Brāhmanas and the Sūtras."[3] Thus the Brāhmanas were composed while Vedic Sanskrit was still the language of the Indo-Aryans. Now Pānini's grammar *deals with classical Sanskrit*, not the Vedic speech. He deals with many points of Vedic grammar, it is true, but he deals with them as exceptions ; his subject is classical Sanskrit. He laid down the law, which has ruled Sanskrit throughout the centuries since his day. Thus he arose at a time, *when the language of the Brāhmanas had become archaic*, and modern Sanskrit had taken its place.[4] It is thus absolutely impossible to believe that Pānini lived and wrote before the Brāhmanas were composed : to propose to put him back before their composition is much the same as proposing to push Johnson's Dictionary back before Chaucer.

Another line of proof may also be indicated. Careful study of the early Brāhmanas has made it plain that they were composed

---

[1] Max Müller, *A. S. L.*, 311-312 ; Macdonell, 36, 39, 268. Cf. what Whitney says, " The standard work of Pānini, the grammarian-in-chief of Sanskrit literature, is a frightfully perfect model of the *Sutra* method " (*Oriental and Linguistic Studies*, I, 71).

[2] Max Muller, *Natural Religion*, 296 ; Macdonell, 203-4.

[3] Macdonell. 205.

[4] Max Müller, *A. S. L.*, 1 ° ; *Natural Religion*, 297-298 ; Macdonell, 22-23.

after the collection of the hymns of the *Rigveda*, but before[1] the formation of the *Sanhitā* text (*i.e.*, the text in which the words are joined according to the rules of *Sandhi*) and the *Pada*[2] text (*i.e.* the word by word text). The author of the *Pada* text is Sākalya.[3] Now Yāska refers to Sākalya as a predecessor ;[4] and Yāska himself is earlier than Pānini.[5] Thus the historical order is the early Brāhmanas, the *Sanhitā* text, Sākalya, Yāska, Pānini.

Bunkim Babu's date for Pānini being thus altogether untenable, his whole argument for the historicity of the *Pāndava Mahābhārata* and Krishna's character as therein pourtrayed tumbles in ruins, and brings down with it all the rest of this Krishna literature.

We would invite our readers to turn away from these vain attempts to turn a myth into sober history, and to listen to the teaching of those really scholarly Indians who study Hinduism from a scientific standpoint. We have already referred to Sitanath Tattvabhushan's *Hindu Theism*, and we have frequently used Bose's *Hindu Civilization under British Rule* and R. C. Dutt's works as authorities. We would now call attention to a monograph by one of the greatest scholars in Bengal (*Comparative Studies in Vaishnavism and Christianity*, by Brajendra Nath Seal), where[6] the growth of the Krishna legend is frankly discussed;[7] also to a very remarkable essay on *Buddhist and Vishnuite* in a recent number of *Sāhitya*[8] by the late Umes Chundra Batabyal, in which grave historical reasons are given for concluding that the *Gītā* is in part at least a polemic against Buddhism ; and to the late Mr. Justice Telang's introduction to his translation of the *Gītā* (*S. B. E*, vol. VIII), with regard to which readers will note, that, although the date is put a little earlier than most scholars would put it, no attempt is made to defend the traditional theory of the origin of the Song.

---

[1] Macdonell, 50.

[2] On these texts see Kaegi, Note 77 ; Macdonell, 48,50.

[3] Macdonell, 51.   [4] Macdonell, 268.

[5] Macdonell, 269. Goldstücker (*op. cit.* p. 225) acknowledges that Yāska earlier than Pānini.

[6] pp. 8-10.   [7] See also Bose, *H. C.*, 33 35.   [8] 13th year, 1-t Part.

Lightning Source UK Ltd.
Milton Keynes UK
UKHW020649210223
417383UK00007B/231